REMEMBERING
THE ARMENIAN GENOCIDE
1915

'... They were only women and children, about two thousand in number. There wasn't one man among them. Terribly emaciated, skin burned brown, clothed in rags, hungry, thirsty, they seemed like madwomen. The dust of the soil was stuck to their faces in such a way that, from a distance, one had the impression of an earthy mass, all stuck one to the other, as if they could never be separated. They were standing there petrified, they didn't know where to go. From time to time a woman sighed, moving her head, or a child fell to the ground, exhausted, and they waited ...'

'... The few men caught alive were taken outside the town and shot. The women and children were either locked in houses in nearby villages and burned to death or drowned in the river ...'

'... At every station where we stopped, we came side by side with one of these trains. It was made up of cattle-trucks, and the faces of little children were looking out from behind the tiny barred windows of each truck. The side-doors were wide open, and one could plainly see old men and old women, young mothers with young babies, men, women and children, all huddled together like so many sheep or pigs...'

Patrick Thomas was born in Welshpool in 1952, and educated at schools in England. He is a graduate of Cambridge and Leeds Universities, and gained his doctorate from the University of Wales. After ordination to the priesthood of the Church in Wales in 1980, he has served his entire ministry in bilingual parishes in West Wales. A member of the Welsh Language Board from 1994 to 2000, he broadcasts regularly in both Welsh and English. He is Vicar of Christ Church, Carmarthen, and Canon Chancellor of St David's Cathedral. He has a deep interest in Armenian history, culture and spirituality, and is a meber of the Anglican-Oriental Orthodox International Commission and honorary pastor to Armenians in Wales.

REMEMBERING
THE ARMENIAN GENOCIDE
1915

Patrick Thomas

By the same author:
Carmarthen to Karabagh: a Welsh discovery of Armenia
Brechfa and Beyond: the peregrinations of a parish priest
Candle in the Darkness: Celtic spirituality from Wales
The Opened Door: a Celtic Spirituality
Celtic Earth, Celitic Heaven:
   saints and heroes of the Powys borderland
Sensuous Glory: The Poetic Vision of D. Gwenallt Jones
   (with Donald Allchin and D. Densil Morgan)
Writers of Wales: Katherine Philips ('Orinda')
The Collected Works of Katherine Philips
   (with Germaine Greer)

First published in 2015

© Patrick Thomas

© Gwasg Carreg Gwalch 2015

ISBN: 978-1-84527-546-4

Published with the financial support
of the Welsh Books Council

Cover Design: Eleri Owen

Published by Gwasg Carreg Gwalch,
12 Iard yr Orsaf, Llanrwst, Conwy, LL26 0EH.
Tel: 01492 642031 Fax: 01492 641502
e-mail: books@carreg-gwalch.com
internet: www.carreg-gwalch.com

Dedicated with respect and friendship
to the Armenians of Wales and Ireland
in memory of the members of their families who perished
in the Genocide of Armenians in Ottoman Turkey
during the First World War

Contents

Introduction

MEDZ YEGHERN ('THE GREAT CRIME')

Anyone who knows anything about the Second World War will be aware of the Holocaust: the Nazi attempt to exterminate the Jews. Comparatively few people, apart from Armenians, are aware of the Genocide that took place in Ottoman Turkey during the First World War. It is estimated that up to a million and a half Armenian Christians perished as a result of a policy of systematic extermination instigated by the leaders of the Ottoman government.

In April 1915 the intellectual, political and cultural leaders of the Armenian community in Constantinople (Istanbul) were deported to the interior, where almost all of them were later killed. Young Armenian men of military age, who had been conscripted to the Turkish army, were disarmed and massacred. Women, children and the elderly were sent on death marches towards the Syrian Desert, during which the vast majority of them perished as a result of starvation, dehydration, disease, brutality and repeated rape. There were also 'killing fields' both in the Armenian Turkish provinces and in the concentration camps established in northern Syria. This was the first large-scale Genocide of the Twentieth Century.

As a result, Armenians were almost entirely eliminated from Western Armenia, the eastern plateau of Ottoman Turkey which had formed part of their homeland for several thousand years. Between the twelfth and the fourteenth centuries there had also been an Armenian Kingdom of Cilicia, between the Taurus Mountains and the Mediterranean Coast. The substantial Armenian community which remained there also became a victim of the Genocide.

Many of the survivors and their descendants were scattered across the Middle East, in Europe (particularly France), the United States and South America, becoming a substantial Armenian diaspora. Those few Armenians who stayed in their traditional heartland became known as 'the leftovers of the sword' by their Turkish neighbours, and often had to lead a furtive and hidden existence.[1] The only sizeable Armenian community that remains in modern-day Turkey is in Istanbul.

Eastern Armenia had been under Russian rule. From 1918 to 1920 it enjoyed a brief and fragile independence, threatened by both resurgent Turkish nationalism and the Soviet Red Army, and overwhelmed by the need to absorb and care for a large number of desperate and starving refugees. Forced to choose between the Turkish crescent and the Bolshevik hammer and sickle, the Armenians opted for the latter, and the country was absorbed into the Soviet Union. In September 1991 Armenia regained its independence.

The twenty first century Republic of Armenia represents about a tenth of what was once Greater Armenia. It is approximately the size of Belgium, and perhaps one-and-a-half times the size of Wales. Today's Armenia is bordered by Turkey, Georgia, Azerbaijan and Iran. Under a deal between the Soviets and the Turks, Mount Ararat, the holy mountain of Armenian culture and tradition, was given to the Turks. The border between Turkey and Armenia is closed. An uneasy cease-fire exists between Armenia and Azerbaijan after a war in the 1990s over the overwhelmingly Armenian-populated province of Nagorno-Karabagh, which is now a self-declared republic.

While the Genocide is seared into the consciousness of every Armenian, most non-Armenians, even if they have some knowledge of the First World War, are unaware of it. I was among them until I discovered Armenia and the Armenians ten years ago. Back in 1965 my father had given me a book by John Terraine: *The Great War 1914-1918: A Pictorial History*. It left no lasting impression of what the Armenians suffered during that conflict. Going back to it recently, I found that they only featured in a single sentence, referring to the German Field Marshal Liman von Sanders: 'His Turkish allies inflamed their martial ardour by the massacre of three-quarters of a million Armenians in their midst.'[2] That statement itself may be open to question by many, both in terms of the number of dead and of the use of the word 'massacre' rather than 'genocide'. It does, however, illustrate the way in which the systematic attempt to destroy the Ottoman Armenians during the First World War has often been kicked into the margins of history.

There are geopolitical and economic reasons why the Genocide has lacked recognition in certain Western countries (notably Britain and the United States). Some of them will emerge in the first chapter of this book. In the Soviet Union there was also a prolonged attempt to sweep the Armenian Genocide under the carpet. An unprecedented mass demonstration held in Yerevan, the Armenian capital, in 1965 forced a rethink, leading to the establishment of the Armenian Genocide Memorial and Museum there. In Turkey itself a growing number of courageous writers and academics have begun to draw people's attention to what really happened to Armenians in their country during the First World War.

The first public memorial in the British Isles to the victims of the Armenian Genocide was unveiled in Cardiff in the garden of the Temple of Peace in 1997. In the years since then, as I have spoken to Welsh and Irish Armenian friends, and heard their family histories (because every Armenian family was touched by the Genocide to some degree), the profound significance of that act of recognition has come home to me. As Roger Smith has pointed out, 'denial ... is the last stage of genocide'.[3] If, even after a hundred years, the reality is denied of an event in which so many people's parents, grandparents, uncles, aunts and other relatives perished, often in a peculiarly cruel and horrific way, the anguish persists and the wound cannot be healed.

This was poignantly confirmed on a recent visit to the Holy Land. A handful of potters in the Armenian quarter of Jerusalem still produce ceramics in the style developed by their ancestors near Constantinople in Ottoman times. A friend introduced me to one of them, telling him that I came from Wales, a country whose National Assembly had recognized the Armenian Genocide. The potter smiled broadly: 'Then you must have this as a present to take home with you.' He pulled a poster from under the counter and handed it to me. It showed a map of Turkish Armenia during the Genocide. Underneath were the words RECOGNITION. CONDEMNATION. PREVENTION.

Recognition of genocide, as the Armenian potter's poster

reminded me, must also lead to condemnation: the attempt to annihilate a people is the most serious of all crimes against humanity. Such recognition and condemnation strengthens the attempt to prevent future genocides in a world that contains so many vulnerable and threatened minorities. Tragically, the twentieth century was a century of genocides, of which the Armenian Genocide was the first major example. We have a moral duty to work together to ensure that our present century does not follow the same pattern.

A few days after my encounter with the Armenian potter, I was sitting in a minibus at the foot of Mount Tabor. Next to me was an Iraqi Armenian woman. She was a descendant of Genocide survivors who had settled in Mosul. That morning we had heard that the city had been seized by the extremist group whose members later proclaimed the 'Islamic State'. My fellow pilgrim told me that she was worried about her brothers and their families who still lived in Mosul. As Christians their lives were in danger. She prayed that they might be able to reach safety in Kurdish held territory.

Returning to Wales, I began work on this book. Whenever I turned on the television news there were stories that seemed to echo the subject of my research and writing. There were references to different groups threatened by genocide: Yazidi, Turkmen and Iraqi Christians. Several of the places mentioned had links with the sufferings of the Armenians in the First World War. One event has a direct link with the horrors of 1915. The northern Syrian town of Der Zor has the same significance for Armenians that Auschwitz has for Jews. The Armenian Apostolic Orthodox church, built there as a memorial to the martyrs of the Genocide, has recently been blown up by Islamic extremists. Its archives have been burned to ashes and the bones of victims, preserved in the crypt, have been thrown into the street.[4]

Either we learn from the tragedies of history, and act on what we learn, or they repeat themselves over and over again. That is why remembering the Armenian Genocide remains important in 2015.

[1] See Laurence Ritter and Max Sivaslian, *Les restes de l'épée: Les Arméniens caches et islamisés de Turquie* (Paris: Editions Thaddée, 2012).

[2] John Terraine, *The Great War 1914-1918: A Pictorial History* (London: Hutchinson, 1965), p.152.

[3] Roger W. Smith, 'The Armenian Genocide: Memory, Politics and the Future' in Richard G. Hovannisian (editor), *The Armenian Genocide: History, Politics, Ethics* (Basingstoke: Macmillan, 1992), p.4.

[4] Robert Fisk, 'Destroyed, the shrine to victims of the Armenian genocide', *The Independent* (11 November 2014), pp.28-9.

Acknowledgements

I am extremely grateful to Myrddin ap Dafydd for undertaking to publish this book, and to Alun Gibbard for his wise editorial guidance. Thanks are also due to John Torosyan for obtaining the photographs and to Ara Sarafian for so generously providing the maps. Without the support and encouragement of Srpazan Hayr Vahan Hovhanessian, formerly Armenian Primate of Britain and Ireland and now Armenian Primate of France, John and Ani Torosyan, Dr Ara and Alice Kanekanian, Dr Paul and Isobel Manook and my many other dear Armenian friends in Wales, Ireland and beyond, this book would not have been written. I would also like to express my sincere thanks to Mr Malcolm Jones for reading through the text before publication, and for his helpful suggestions.

A glance at the footnotes will reveal my indebtedness to some remarkable scholars and historians: Ara Sarafian, Raymond Kévorkian, Wolfgang Gust, Vahakn Dadrian, Taner Akçam, Verjiné Svazlian, Richard Hovannisian and many others, as well as those survivors and witnesses who ensured that the horrifying reality of the Armenian Genocide was not forgotten.

Bishop Wyn Evans is remarkably tolerant towards one of the most eccentric of his clergy. I am not sure how he has put up with me over the years, but am thankful that he has done so. The same is true of Dean Jonathan Lean, who allows me to devote myself to research and writing during my annual stint at the Cathedral, when I should really be making polite conversation to visitors. Equally long-suffering are my amazingly patient wife, Helen, and our children, and my wonderful church members and colleagues in ministry in Carmarthen (who probably know more about

Armenia and Armenians by now than almost anyone else in the Anglican Communion).

This book is intended as a personal expression of respect for the Armenian people and an acknowledgment of their appalling suffering during the Genocide that began in 1915. No doubt it contains mistakes and omissions, and for these I sincerely apologize.

A Note on Transliteration

I have attempted to standardize the spelling of names and places in the text. I have usually, though not always, copied the forms used in the *UCLA Armenian History and Culture Series: Historic Armenian Cities and Provinces*. Where passages are quoted, the spelling used by the author of the quotation is retained. Thus, for example, the American missionaries tended to write 'Harpoot' or 'Harput' for 'Kharpert','Ourfa' for 'Urfa' and 'Moush' or 'Moosh' for 'Mush'. I have chosen to use 'Constantinople' rather than 'Istanbul' and 'Smyrna' rather than 'Izmir' whenever that seems most appropriate. The difference in transliteration between Western and Eastern Armenian also has an impact on the spelling of personal names. I have tried to reflect the forms most commonly used in my sources: 'Komitas' rather than 'Gomidas', to give one obvious example. I hope that the result is relatively easy to follow.

The Armenian Genocide: A Summary

Before the First World War, Armenians formed a substantial minority within multi-racial Ottoman Turkey. They had been the victims of massacres in 1895-6 and 1909, which had outraged public opinion in Europe and America. In 1913 Turkey and Russia agreed to appoint inspectors general to oversee the administration of the six provinces with the largest Armenian population. A Dutchman and a Norwegian were appointed to these posts, but never took them up because of the outbreak of war.

European interference on their behalf increased antipathy towards Armenians among 'Young Turk' politicians. The Armenian middle class of professional people, successful merchants and craftsmen were often envied for their wealth. The loss of territory in Europe during the Balkan wars and the resulting influx of refugees led to pressure to ethnically cleanse and 'Turkify' the remaining Asian provinces. The division of historic Armenia between Turkey and Russia also led some Turks to regard their Armenian fellow citizens as a potentially subversive 'fifth column'.

When the Ottoman Empire allied itself with Germany and Austria-Hungary in 1914, the Turkish Armenians pledged their allegiance to the Sultan (though a small number defected to join the Russian Armenian militias). Armenian men of military age were conscripted to the Turkish army. However they were later disarmed and turned into labour battalions. These were then slaughtered in batches, often having to dig their own graves.

In March 1915 the population of the semi-autonomous and fiercely independent Armenian stronghold of Zeytun were persuaded by their religious leader to give up their arms and submit to being deported. In the major Armenian centre of Van the Turkish governor arranged the murder of leading Armenians and instigated massacres in surrounding villages. The Armenians of Van defended themselves, holding out until they were relieved by the Russian army.

The 24 April 1915 is remembered as the date on which the Genocide began to be implemented. The Armenian community in Constantinople was effectively 'beheaded' by the sudden arrest of its cultural, political and intellectual leaders, who were deported into the interior. Only a tiny handful of them survived. In many other centres leading Armenians were rounded up, brutally tortured and killed.

A 'Special Organization' of criminals (including many convicted murderers) had been recruited from the prisons. They were sent to the provinces to enforce the deportation of Armenians, with the assistance of Kurdish irregulars. In the Armenian heartland these deportations usually followed a set pattern. The remaining men would be rounded up, taken away and massacred. The women and children were sent on death marches towards the Syrian desert. Many were gang-raped, some were abducted or trafficked, while others were left to die of exhaustion or starvation at the side of the road. Pregnant women had the babies ripped from their wombs. Those suspected of swallowing gold coins were sometimes set on fire. Their ashes were later sifted by those looking for loot. In Trebizond boatloads of Armenians were taken out and drowned in the Black Sea.

Few survived the death marches. A later phase of deportation included the transportation by rail of Armenians from Western Turkey, crammed into cattle trucks. Insanitary transit camps were set up, where many perished from disease. Those who reached the concentration camps in Northern Syria were later brutally eliminated. In a few places Armenians refused to hand in their arms and attempted resistance, only to be overwhelmed and slaughtered. At Musa Dagh on the Mediterranean coast, however, a courageous band of Armenian villagers held off a Turkish attack during a lengthy siege, and were eventually rescued by French naval vessels. The penalty for a Turk found sheltering an Armenian was death by hanging. Nevertheless some Turks and Kurds did take the risk of helping their Armenian neighbours. Those brave officials who refused to implement their government's genocidal plans were almost all either removed or assassinated.

Evidence for the Armenian Genocide is overwhelming. It comes from eye-witness accounts by survivors, accounts of the trials of some of the perpetrators that took place immediately after the end of the war, reports by missionaries, diplomats and foreign soldiers and railway officials working alongside the Turks. Although attempts were made to ensure that no photographic evidence would survive, horrified observers like the German medical orderly Armin Wegner managed to smuggle out pictures of some of the atrocities. Perhaps the most damning evidence of all is the fact that those areas of Western Turkey which were the homeland of Armenians for thousands of years now form an Armenia without Armenians.

Who's Who: A Select Guide

TURKS

Abdul Hamid II was Sultan of the Ottoman Empire from 1876 to 1909. He was responsible for the massacre of between 100,000 and 200,000 Armenians in 1896. After being implicated in an attempted counter-revolution by reactionaries against the Young Turks, he was deposed in 1909.

Ahmet Refik was a distinguished historian and former teacher of Mustafa Kemal (Atatürk). In 1918 he described the treatment of the Armenians as 'a crime against humanity'.

Ahmet Riza was a prominent Turkish politician who openly opposed the anti-Armenian policy of the government in 1915. In 1918 he declared that the Armenians had been 'subject to atrocities that are unparalleled in Ottoman history'.

Dr Behaeddin Shakir was Director of the Special Organization formed of released convicts and Kurdish tribesmen. It was used to implement the worst horrors of the Armenian Genocide. He was assassinated in Berlin in 1922.

Djemal Pasha was a member of the ruling triumvirate of the Young Turk Committee of Union and Progress. He took over power in the Ottoman Empire (with Enver and Talaat) in 1913, becoming Minister of the Navy. He was assassinated in Tiflis (Tbilisi) in 1922.

Enver Pasha was another member of the Young Turk triumvirate, serving as Minister of War. He modelled himself on Napoleon, without much success. Enver blamed the Armenians for his disastrous campaign in the Caucasus (where an Armenian soldier saved his life). He became a strong supporter of the forceful implementation of the

Genocide. Enver was killed at Bukhara in 1922 during a skirmish with the Red Army.

Mustafa Kemal (Atatürk) was the hero of the Dardanelles, leader of the Turkish nationalist resurgence after the defeat in World War I and architect of the modern Turkish state. He was an advocate of 'Turkification', but described the treatment of Ottoman Armenians during World War I as 'a shameful act'.

Reshid Bey was governor of the 'slaughterhouse province' of Mamuret-ul-Aziz (Diarbekir), where some of the worst atrocities of the Armenian Genocide took place.

Salih Zeki Bey was governor of Der Zor in the deserts of northern Syria in 1916. He was responsible for cruelty and massacres on a massive scale.

Talaat Bey (Talaat Pasha from 1917) was the man principally responsible for planning and implementing the Armenian Genocide. He kept a notebook containing statistics of the annihilations. A telegraph operator by training, he used this experience to coordinate the slaughter of Armenians. Talaat seized power as with Enver and Djemal in 1913 and was Minister of the Interior until 1917, when he became Grand Vizier. He resigned in 1918 and fled to Berlin, where he was assassinated in 1921. His body was returned to Turkey by the Nazis in 1943 and was given a hero's funeral.

GERMANS

Ernst Jakob Christoffel was head of the German Home for the Blind in Malatia. He was devastated by the impact of the Genocide.

Franz Johannes Günther was the Constantinople-based Vice-President of the Anatolian Railway and Chairman of the Baghdad Railway. Although unsympathetic towards Armenians, he was highly critical of their treatment by the Turkish authorities.

Johannes Lepsius was a missionary and an advocate of the Turkish Armenians. He was regarded as an embarrassment by the German authorities.

Otto Liman von Sanders was head of the German Military Mission in Turkey from 1913.

Siegfried Graf von Lüttichau was the preacher at the German Embassy in Constantinople who was sent to investigate the impact of the Turkish annihilation of Armenians.

Walter Rössler was the German Consul in Aleppo. He was sympathetic towards the suffering Armenians and critical of Turkish policy.

Max Erwin von Scheubner-Richter was the German Deputy Consul in Erzerum. A founder member of the Nazi party, he was shot in 1923 while marching at Hitler's side.

Hans Freiherr von Wangenheim was the German Ambassador in Constantinople. He was probably the only person who was influential enough to stop the Genocide, but tragically he was hostile towards the Armenians.

Eberhard Count Wolffskeel von Reichenberg was a Bavarian captain serving with the Turkish Fourth Army. He directed the Turkish artillery during the siege of the Armenian quarter of Urfa.

ARMENIANS

Manoug Adoian was an adolescent at the time of the Genocide, taking part in the self-defence of Armenian Van. Moving to America, he became the artist 'Arshile Gorky'. His childhood and teenage experiences influenced his painting.

Aram Andonian was an author and journalist arrested during the purge of Constantinople's Armenian elite on 24 April 1915. Because of an accident, he survived the massacre of his companions, and wrote of his experiences during the Genocide.

Dikran Andreasian was the Protestant pastor in Zeytun. After the people of Zeytun were the first to be deported, he was allowed to return to his home town of Musa Dagh, and played an important role in its defence.

Father Grigoris Balakian was a celibate Armenian Apostolic priest in Constantinople. He was a survivor of the 24 April arrests, and author of *Armenian Golgotha*, an important memoir of the Genocide. After the First World War he became the Armenian Bishop in Manchester.

Eghishe Charents was a young Eastern Armenian volunteer, fighting alongside the Russians. Eye-witness descriptions of massacred Armenians appear in his long poem 'Dantesque Legend'.

Komitas (Gomidas) Vartabed was a celibate Armenian Apostolic priest, who was also the leading Armenian musicologist, composer and collector of folk songs. He was arrested on 24 April 1915, but later freed as a result of the American Ambassador's intervention. Traumatized by his experiences, he was confined in mental hospitals from 1916 until his death in 1935.

Aram Manukian was the leader of the successful defence of the Armenian areas of Van in 1915. He organized the defence of Yerevan in 1918, but died of typhus early in the following year.

Arshaluys (Aurora) Mardiganian was the seventeen-year-old star of the American silent film *Ravished Armenia/ Auction of Souls*, based on her appalling experiences during her deportation, abduction and eventual escape between 1915 and 1917.

Hayg Toroyan was a witness to the treatment of Armenian deportees in Aleppo and the concentration camps on the Euphrates. His experiences were dictated to the Armenian writer **Zabel Yesayan (Essayan)**, while both were refugees in the Caucasus.

Vartkes (Hovhannes Serengiulian) was the Dashnak (Armenian Revolutionary Federation) deputy for Erzerum in the Ottoman Parliament. He was betrayed by Talaat, whom he had once regarded as a close friend, arrested and brutally murdered in 1915.

Krikor Zohrab was a Liberal deputy for Constantinople in the Ottoman Parliament. He was a distinguished lawyer and legislator, and a gifted writer of short stories. He stood up for the Armenians against Talaat, his former friend. He was murdered with Vartkes in 1915.

AMERICANS

Dr Tacy W. Atkinson was a medical missionary in Kharpert (Harpoot) with her husband, who died of typhus there. She kept a diary during the Genocide.

Leslie A. Davis was the American Consul in Kharpert (Harpoot) from 1915 to 1917. He was an important witness to the impact of the Genocide on the 'slaughterhouse province' of Ottoman Armenia.

Henry Morgenthau was American Ambassador in Constantinople. A naturalized American from a German Jewish background, he worked tirelessly to try to change Talaat and Enver's policy towards the Armenians. Morgenthau also helped to bring Armenian suffering to the attention of the United States and the rest of the world.

Bertha Morley was a missionary in Marsovan during the Genocide. She kept a diary that throws light on the Genocide.

Henry Riggs was a missionary at Kharpert (Harpoot) during the Genocide. He was the author of *Days of Tragedy in Armenia*, a substantial first-hand account of the events there between 1915 and 1917.

Dr Clarence D. Ussher was a medical missionary at Van. His autobiography, *An American Physician in Turkey*, contains a description of the siege of the Armenian areas of Van.

OTHERS

Maria Jacobsen came from Denmark. She was a missionary in Kharpert (Harpoot) from 1907 to 1919. Her diaries contain invaluable insights into the nature of the Genocide.

Alma Johansson was a Swedish national working with the German mission in Mush. Her observations on the Genocide, and the events leading up to it, are particularly significant.

Raphael Lemkin was a Polish Jewish lawyer, whose reflections on the treatment of Ottoman Armenians in the First World War started him on the journey that eventually led him to coin the word 'genocide'.

Rafael de Nogales was a Venezuelan mercenary who became an officer in the Ottoman army, serving at the siege of Van and in the Ottoman Armenian provinces at the height of the Genocide. His memoirs, *Four Years Beneath the Crescent*, contain descriptions of both the perpetrators and their victims.

Beatrice Rohner was a Swiss missionary who observed the appalling conditions of Armenians in the camp at Meskené.

Franz Werfel was the Austrian Jewish author of *The Forty Days of Musa Dagh*, perhaps the most famous novel about the Armenian Genocide.

1. THE AIRBRUSHING OF HISTORY

THE PASTOR'S MISSION

The perpetrators of genocide have every reason to cover their traces. Independent witnesses to atrocities are therefore particularly important for anyone who wishes to uncover the truth of what has taken place. In the case of the Armenian Genocide reports by foreign diplomats and missionaries have a special significance in confirming the evidence from Armenian survivors.

Because Germany and Turkey were close allies throughout the First World War, evidence from German sources plays a key role in establishing the nature and extent of the Armenian Genocide. As the conflict ground inexorably towards its close, the Germans were worried that they might be accused of involvement in the Ottoman government's attempt to wipe out its Armenian subjects. They were concerned that this would certainly have an impact on the terms of any future peace settlement.

Between May and August 1918 the German Embassy in

Constantinople (Istanbul) despatched its chaplain, the aristocratic Pastor Siegfied Graf von Lüttichau, on a fact-finding tour. As he travelled through eastern Turkey his focus was on provinces which for centuries had been a part of the Armenian heartland. During his journey he interviewed eye witnesses of the catastrophic and systematic slaughter of Armenians that had begun in 1915, and that, as he remarked, was 'still not finished'.

Karl Axenfeld, the Director of the Orient and Islam Commission of the German Protestant Mission Board, passed Lüttichau's report on to the German Foreign Office in October 1918. Axenfeld expressed his concern that Britain and France and their allies, as well as a great many Turks, would try to blame the German government for the fate of the Armenians. He was aware that 'we German Christians are also being accused abroad that, due to the blindness caused by the war and our national egoism, we indifferently and lethargically ignored the greatest murder of Christians of all times'.[1] The Embassy Pastor's report was being published to counteract this accusation.

It was true that German official policy had long been either antagonistic or indifferent towards the Armenians. In 1896 the 'Red Sultan' Abdul Hamid orchestrated the massacre of over a hundred thousand of his Armenian subjects, to the horror of most of Europe. Baron Alfons Mumm von Scharzenstein, the German Office advisor for Near Eastern Affairs had, however, described these 'bloodbaths' as 'regrettable', and then declared that 'Germany has no grounds to intervene on behalf of a race in which she has absolutely no interest ...'[2] That attitude would persist at the highest level during the First World War.

In December 1915, Wolff-Metternich, the German Ambassador in Constantinople, contacted Berlin. He was far more sympathetic towards the Armenians than his predecessor, Wangenheim, who had dismissed them as 'nothing but treacherous vermin'.[3] The new ambassador asked the German government to draw the attention of the Turkish government publicly to the 'deeply unfortunate events which have occurred during the relocation of the Armenians in Turkey' and to demand that the 'excesses and harshness' be immediately stopped. Bethmann Hollweg, the German Imperial Chancellor, bluntly dismissed Metternich's 'proposed reprimand of an ally during a war'. He described it as 'unprecedented in history', and went on to state firmly that the German government's 'only aim is to keep Turkey on our side until the end of the war, no matter whether as a result Armenians do perish or not'.[4]

There is no doubt that, while the Genocide was taking place, many of those in the areas most affected suspected some kind of German involvement. Tacy Atkinson, an American missionary, had been in Kharpert (Harpoot) since 1909. The deportation of Armenians from the town was announced on 10 July 1915. She made an entry in her diary that day, which she then realized was so potentially dangerous that she carefully crossed it out. Modern scientific techniques, however, have now enabled it to be deciphered. It included a reference to Pastor Johannes Ehmann, the local German missionary:

Among the Turks and Armenians both it seems pretty well known that this thing is from the Germans. Even Mr. Ehman himself is coming to the conviction that it is the work of his own government. We all know such clear-cut, well planned, all well carried out work is not the method of the Turk. The German, the Turk and the devil made a triple alliance not to be equalled in the world for cold blooded hellishness.[5]

Two days later, during the deportations from Marsovan, Bertha Morley, another American missionary, noted that 'some Turks are saying in the city that they and their religion would never do anything as cruel as this, that it must be Germany and Christianity'.[6]

In reality the German involvement was rather more complicated. Many of the German missionaries, soldiers, railway workers, merchants and consular officials were sympathetic towards the Armenians, particularly when the horrifying fate faced by the deported Armenian women and children became clear. Others were hostile. One, a certain Lieutenant-Colonel Böttrich, Director of Railways of the Anatolian Railway Company, went so far as to put his signature to an order endorsing the deportation of Armenian railway workers. The company's deputy director in Constantinople was furious. He wrote to his superiors in Berlin that a time would come when Germany's enemies would be willing to pay a substantial sum for the bit of paper signed by Böttrich, because they would be able to use it to 'prove that not only did the Germans do nothing to prevent the persecution of the Armenians, but that certain orders towards this objective were even sent out (i.e., signed by them)'.[7]

Two of the key German figures involved in the Turkish war effort reveal the ambiguous nature of their country's position. Vahakn Dadrian describes a lecture given by General Colmar von der Goltz to the German-Turkish League in Berlin in February 1914. Its audience included representatives from the Turkish Embassy. Among the general's propositions was the suggestion that the Armenians from the Russo-Turkish border provinces of Van, Bitlis and Erzerum should be transplanted to Aleppo and Mesopotamia. The Arabs of the latter areas would then be moved to the Russo-Turkish border.[8] This moving around of large numbers of people as though they were pawns in a chess game was a bit of military theorizing which the Turkish leaders would later extend and develop with horrific results.

Count von Lüttischau noted in his report that Field Marshal von der Goltz had seen and approved the much more vague and elastic proposal made by the Turkish Government. To the Embassy preacher, 'the official version looked harmless enough'. It gave army commanders 'in case of military necessity, and in case they suspect espionage and treason' the power 'to deport individual or groups of inhabitants in villages or towns and resettle them in other places'.[9] Interestingly enough, it was another leading German general who questioned the way in which the Turkish authorities were interpreting this clause, and thereby succeeded in helping to save (at least for a few years) the Armenian population of one of Turkey's most significant cities.

The Turkish governor of Smyrna (Izmir), Rahmi Bey, had been unwilling to allow the deportation of the Armenians of his province, much to the annoyance of Talaat, the Minister of the Interior and one of the moving spirits behind the Genocide. Two foreign observers who met Rahmi in September 1915 spoke very highly of him. Henry Morgenthau, the American ambassador, noted in his diary that he 'seems to me to be one of the forceful and intelligent men that I have met'. Tyska, a German journalist, regarded him as more cosmopolitan than Talaat, describing Rahmi as having 'a practical, but also humane character'. A recent commentator calls him 'forward-thinking and prudent'.[10]

Despite his attempts to protect the Armenians, Rahmi Bey came under increasing pressure both from the local branch of the Committee for Union and Progress (the

Young Turk political party, usually referred to as the CUP) and from Talaat in Constantinople. Eventually the governor was forced to give in. The first deportation of Armenian families from Smyrna took place on 9 November 1916. Count Spee, the German Consul General there, telegraphed the Embassy in Constantinople the following day: 'Germany's reputation seriously endangered'. He expanded on this shortly afterwards:

> The government's measures were carried out at a time when, apart from the Commander of the German Corps, the Commander-in-Chief, Marshal Liman von Sanders, was also in Smyrna. There is a rumour in town that the Germans had prepared the procedure in order to rid themselves in this way of the Armenian competition that was inconvenient for their trade.

Liman von Sanders reacted angrily to this slur. He told the governor that 'as such mass deportations infringe on the military sector ... without my permission, such mass arrests and deportations would no longer be allowed to take place'. He threatened to use military force to prevent any repetition of the situation. The governor gave in, saying that he had only been following Talaat's orders. The deportees were allowed home and the Armenians of Smyrna were saved, though tragically a large number of them would die during the Kemalist capture of the city in 1922.[11]

Talaat was deeply disappointed by the result of the German intervention in Smyrna/Izmir. On a visit to the city's Sporting Club he apparently remarked to İhsan Ohnik, the local parliamentary deputy, that 'I would have subjected the ones here [i.e. the Armenians of Izmir] to the same fate as the ones there [in Anatolia]'.[12] The Smyrna intervention suggests that sufficient German pressure from the right quarter might possibly have limited or even halted the Armenian Genocide.

In July 1915 Ambassador Wangenheim reported to Berlin that 'the expulsion and relocation of the Armenians' had been extended from the war zone to three other provinces with substantial Armenian populations, even though these parts of the country are not threatened by any enemy invasion for the time being'. He concluded that 'the government is indeed pursuing its purpose of eradicating the Armenian race from the Turkish Empire'. He personally handed the Ottoman Grand Vizier a memorandum which was intended 'to effectively counteract any possible later invectives on the part of our enemies, as if we were jointly to blame for the rigorous Turkish actions'. This diplomatic fig leaf stated that the German government 'can only approve of the deportation of the Armenian people if it is carried out as a result of military considerations and serves as a security against revolts'. Wangenheim added that 'in carrying out these measures one should provide protection for the deportees against plundering and butchery'.[13]

As far as the American Ambassador Henry Morgenthau was concerned, Wangenheim's words were simply 'a paper protest' that would be wholly ineffectual. He told his German colleague that, although Germany had not instigated the massacre of the Armenians, 'she is responsible in the sense that she had the power to stop them and did not use it'.[14] Count von Lüttichau, writing as the end of the war approached, saw things differently. He claimed that 'Germany has protested long enough and strongly enough: to the Sublime Porte [the seat of the Ottoman government], but not in public'. His view was that the Turkish authorities themselves had been responsible for giving the impression that the Germans were in favour of their treatment of the Armenians.

The Embassy preacher referred to a speech made by Hashim Bey, the parliamentary deputy of Malatia, when he returned home from Constantinople 'in the late autumn of 1915 or spring of 1916'. The politician had gathered all the leading figures in the community together. According to Count von Lüttichau's informant, who had been present at the meeting, the deputy had told them that he had been present when 'the German Ambassador appeared at the Sublime Porte to pass on official congratulations in the name of his government to the Imperial Ottoman government on the extensive implementation and excellent success of the annihilation of the Armenian people'. The 'congratulations' were, of course, a fiction ('such shamelessness exceeds all limits', harrumphed the Count). The extensive annihilation was a grim, appalling fact.

GENOCIDE: 'ANNIHILATION OF THE RACE'

Wiping out the Armenians was a project dear to Talaat's heart. At the height of the killing in 1915, Rafael de Nogales, a colourful Venezuelan mercenary who had obtained a commission in the Ottoman army, met Reshid Bey, the notoriously brutal governor of Diarbekir. In the ensuing conversation Reshid named the person who was to blame for the horrors which the Armenians had suffered. Nogales recorded in his memoirs:

> ... through some exceedingly prudent but very explicit remarks, he gave me to understand also that, in regard to the extermination of the Armenians of his vilayet [province], he had merely obeyed superior orders; so that the responsibility for the massacres perpetrated there should not rest with him, but with his chief, the

Minister of the Interior, Talaat Bey – one year later the Grand Vizier, Talaat Pasha. Talaat had ordered the slaughter by a circular telegram, if my memory is correct, containing a scant three words: '*Yak – Vur – Oldur*,' meaning 'Burn, demolish, kill.'[15]

A notebook has survived in which Talaat attempted to work out, as far as was possible, the numerical impact of his policies on the Armenian population. His conclusion was that approximately 1,150,000 Ottoman Armenians (77% of the total) had vanished between 1914 and 1917.[16]

Count von Lüttichau noted that Walter Rössler, the German Consul in Aleppo, a constant critic of Turkish actions against the Armenians, suggested the figure of one million. Ernst Jakob Christoffel, the head of the German Home for the Blind in Malatia, thought the Armenian losses were considerably greater. In April 1916 he had written from Sivas to Consul General Mordtmann in Constantinople:

> There were 500 men in a village near Sivas with which I have good relations; 30 of them are still alive. A family of 18 lost 14 of its members through sickness and murder. Out of other large families, one or 2 members are still alive. These are not isolated cases, but rather the rule. The number of those killed can be inferred from this. There is great misery in Malatia, as many children and women of those deported remained there. However, the number has been greatly decimated by epidemics and hunger. I am afraid of the task that awaits me there. Nor are the Protestants spared. May the Lord God soon show mercy.[17]

The devout and sensitive missionary was overwhelmed by the horrors that he had seen. In March 1917 he had the opportunity to send an uncensored letter via a visitor to a colleague in Berlin. In it Christoffel wrote that 'the losses to the Armenian people during the period since the deportation until today have surpassed 2 million'. As for 'the last wretched few of the deported ... their numbers are decreasing daily due to disease and forced conversions'. He spoke of 'the complete annihilation of a Christian nation' and asked if the German Protestant Church, celebrating the four hundredth anniversary of the Reformation, would 'have no word of protest about the fact that a sister church was destroyed by sadistic fanatics?'[18]

Count von Lüttichau avoided numerical estimates of the number of Armenian dead or disappeared. Instead he thought it more sensible to work out the losses as percentages of the Armenians from each area. His calmly stated conclusion was profoundly shocking:

> In the eastern provinces, that is excluding Constantinople and Smyrna and other places in Western Turkey, 80-90% of the entire [Armenian] population and 98% of the male [Armenian] population is no longer alive. These figures are probably correct. They can be checked town by town and correspond to my personal impressions and observations.

When he took into account those areas of Western Turkey where Armenians had also been driven out, the Count's final suggestion was that 'in total at least 80% of the [Armenian] population was annihilated'.[19] This is remarkably close to the estimate of 77% which Talaat had made a year earlier (during that extra year many more deportees would, of course, have died).

It had become apparent back as early as May 1915 that what was taking place in the Ottoman Empire was systematic extermination of a completely different kind and scale to previous horrors that had been inflicted on the Armenians. Britain, France and Russia issued a joint declaration on 24 May:

> For approximately one month, the Kurdish and Turkish population of Armenia have acted in collusion, often with the support of the Ottoman Authorities, to massacre the Armenians ... In the face of these new crimes of Turkey against humanity and civilization, the allied Governments are letting the Sublime Porte know publicly that they will hold personally responsible for those crimes all members of the Ottoman Government, as well as those of its agents who will be found implicated in similar massacres.[20]

Vahakn Dadrian has noted that this declaration 'introduced, and thus promulgated for the first time as a general principle of law, the term "crimes against humanity"'.[21]

Another person who had been involved, like Count von Lüttichau, in an investigation in the Armenian provinces in the summer of 1918, was the distinguished Turkish historian Professor Ahmet Refik, who had taught history to Mustafa Kemal (Atatürk) at the War Staff College in Istanbul. His original brief was to examine some reprisals committed by Armenians against Turks in January and February 1918. This, however, led him to consider the mass murders that had sparked such revenge attacks. Refik wrote that the 'CUP was intent on eradicating the Armenians and thereby eliminating the [vexing] Eastern Question'. He noted the use of the *çetes* (irregulars), 'thieves and murderers ... released from the prisons', used by the Special Organization to perpetrate 'the greatest crimes' against the Armenians. Refik concluded his comments on the atrocities by also speaking of 'the entire undertaking' as 'a crime against humanity'. He added that 'No government, at no time, has ever acted with such perfidy and cruelty.'[22]

The word 'genocide' would not be coined until 1944. The *Shorter Oxford English Dictionary* defines it as 'annihilation of the race'. Although the actual term 'genocide' had not yet been defined, the concept of racial annihilation was used at an early stage in the atrocities to describe what was being done to the Ottoman Armenians. On 3 July 1915, Bertha Morley wrote in her diary, after recording a Turkish official's comments on the deportation and killing of Armenians: 'It looks as if the crushing or annihilation of the race were aimed at'.[23] Two months later Herr Kuckhoff, the Honorary German Consul in Samsun on the Black Sea coast, remarked bitterly to the German Embassy in Constantinople:

> Nebuchadnezzar and Abdul Hamid were good-natured people, pure bunglers as far as their talent for annihilation was concerned, for neither they nor Genghis Khan, Tamerlane and the old Turkish sultans managed to completely eradicate with such success a people spread out over a wide country within a few weeks, as we are now experiencing with a shudder.[24]

Another German who used the word 'annihilation' was Franz Johannes Günther, chairman of the Baghdad Railway in Constantinople. After travelling through areas which were being ethnically cleansed of Armenians, he wrote a report for the German Embassy marked 'Strictly Confidential!' describing some of what he had witnessed. Writing of his personal attitude towards the Armenians, Günther confessed that 'I am no friend of what, to me, is a very dislikeable people'. This racist lack of natural sympathy gives a curious authority to his assertion that 'there are definite signs that the Armenians in the east ... are systematically being completely slaughtered ... we are confronted with the annihilation of a people comparable only to the Roman Bar Kokhba Wars against the Jewish people'.[25]

If observers like the neutral American missionary, and two of Turkey's German allies, the Honorary Consul and the racially prejudiced railway chairman, regarded the treatment of the Armenians as 'annihilation', it may not be surprising that a Turkish military leader shared the same view. In 1918 General Khalil informed his German chief of staff that the 'total annihilation of the Armenian race' was about to solve 'the Armenian question'.[26] Such statements destroy the slightest doubt that the Armenians were the subject of genocide during the First World War.

In the immediate aftermath of the war some Turkish politicians were willing to concede the true nature of the crime that had been committed. Senate President Ahmet Riza declared that the Armenians had been 'subjected to atrocities that are unparalleled in Ottoman history'. Riza possessed the moral authority to make this statement. Between October and December 1915 he had spoken out in the Senate on four occasions, openly criticizing the policy of Talaat, the architect of the Genocide, and pleading for mercy to be shown to the Armenians.[27]

The genocidal nature of the treatment of the Ottoman Armenians was clearly expressed in a report made by Dr Martin Niepage, a German assistant master in Aleppo, which was passed on to the German Chancellor in August 1916. The schoolmaster viewed the deportations as an action intended to bring about 'the extinction of the entire Armenian people'. He saw proof of this in the way in which the Turkish government was stopping 'missions, merciful nuns and Europeans who live in the country' from giving any assistance to the deportees. He mentioned in particular a Swiss engineer who 'was to be court-martialled because he distributed bread in Anatolia to the starving women and children of a deportation convoy'.[28]

After the defeat of both Turkey and Germany, Mustafa Arif, whose post as Minister of the Interior had been held by Talaat at the height of the genocide, roundly condemned his predecessor. He wrote in a newspaper article:

> ... it is incumbent upon a government to pursue only guilty ones. Unfortunately our wartime leaders, imbued with a spirit of brigandage, carried out the law of deportation in a manner that would surpass the proclivities of the most bloodthirsty brigands. They decided to exterminate the Armenians, and they did exterminate them. This decision was taken by the Central Committee of the Young Turks and was implemented by the government.

A few days later he created uproar in the Chamber of Deputies by stating that 'the atrocities against the Armenians reduced our country to a gigantic slaughterhouse.' The attempts of the Young Turk CUP deputies to shout him down came to nothing when Arif suddenly read out the Sultan's rescript dissolving the chamber.[29] The repercussions of Talaat and his henchmen's attempt to annihilate the Armenians had come to the forefront of the Turkish domestic political agenda, largely because of the potential impact on a future peace settlement with the victorious allies.

'WHO, AFTER ALL, SPEAKS TODAY OF THE ANNIHILATION OF THE ARMENIANS?'

In October 1919 Major General James Harbord, who had led an American fact-finding mission to Armenia, submitted its report to the United States Congress. The General was appalled by what he had discovered. 'Mutilation, violation, torture, and death have left their haunting memories in a hundred beautiful Armenian valleys, and the traveller in that region is seldom free from the evidence of this most colossal crime of all the ages', he told congressmen.[30] Yet only twenty years later this 'most colossal crime of all the ages' seemed to have been airbrushed out of history.

On 22 August 1939, on the threshold of the Second World War, Adolf Hitler addressed a meeting of his Supreme Commanders and Commanding Generals at Obersalzburg. He told them:

> ... I have placed my death-head formations in readiness – for the present only in the East – with orders to them to send to death mercilessly and without compassion, men, women, and children of Polish derivation and language. Only thus shall we gain the living space (Lebensraum) that we need. Who, after all, speaks today of the annihilation of the Armenians?[31]

Although Hitler inflicted appalling suffering on the Poles, his genocidal policies soon focussed on the Jews. In 1943, when the true horror of what was taking place was beginning to become apparent, the Jewish journalist Shlomo Gross wrote that 'the German regime has brought on Continental Europe's Jewry a Holocaust that has no parallel except the Holocaust brought on the Armenian nation during World War I'.[32] Gross realized that the attempted extermination of the Armenians had provided Hitler with both a precedent and a blueprint for his own appalling scheme.

Several factors were responsible for the way in which the subject of the Armenian Genocide was swept under the carpet during the period between the two world wars. On 28 July 1915 the British House of Lords held a debate on the 'Reported Massacres in Armenia'. Viscount Bryce suggested that the Turkish Government might somehow be informed, perhaps through the American Embassy in Constantinople, 'that their conduct now could not fail to be remembered and would affect whatever action the Allied Powers might take at the conclusion of the war'.[33] The Allies had already issued the declaration a couple of months before which spoke of 'new crimes of Turkey against humanity and civilisation', stating that those implicated in such crimes, including members of the Government, would be held personally responsible for their misdoings. The difficulty that faced the victorious Allies at the end of the First World War was that there was no framework of international law under which those who had been involved in annihilating the Armenians could be tried.

The only leverage which the Allies possessed was the possibility that a failure to prosecute the mass murderers would have an impact on the peace settlement that was still to be agreed with Turkey. With the prospect of this Sword of Damocles (linked to the potential threat of the dismemberment of Asia Minor and the internationalization of Constantinople) hanging over it, the Ottoman Government set up a Special Military Tribunal to hold a series of courts-martial to try some of the principal suspects. Vahakn Dadrian points out that this was 'an unprecedented event in several respects'. The Government was admitting that organized atrocities on a vast scale had taken place, and that the crimes should be fully and properly investigated and those responsible punished, even if they were at the highest level of government or of the Young Turk Committee of Union and Progress.[34]

The contrast with the aftermath of the killing of over 20,000 Armenians in Adana in 1909 could not have been clearer. In a protest to the Ottoman foreign minister after that atrocity, the French ambassador noted that 'the court-martial has largely adopted the version of events put forward by the Adana authorities, who wanted to pin the blame for the catastrophe on the Armenians'. The result was that six Armenians and nine Muslims were hanged. The ambassador described the latter as 'merely tools of no real importance'. The local instigators of the mass killings were all acquitted, and the idea that Armenians could be massacred with impunity was thus strengthened.[35] It was a belief that had already been given substance by the official reaction to the devastating pogroms of Armenians under Sultan Abdul Hamid II in 1894-6.

The major trials conducted by the Special Military Tribunal are of particular importance because, as Dadrian notes, 'the verdicts depended almost entirely on Muslim testimony supporting the bulk of the existing documentary evidence'.[36] This makes them a stumbling block (one of many) for those who still attempt to deny the Armenian Genocide. In the end the Istanbul Number One Extraordinary Court sentenced eighteen people to death for their part in the attempted destruction of the Armenians. In fact, this tally is not quite as impressive or draconian as it may at first seem. Fifteen of the convicted men were tried in their absence. Only three were actually hanged. A British official commented wryly that 'the sentences have been apportioned among the absent and present so as to effect a minimum of real bloodshed'.[37]

The first of the condemned to be executed was Mehmet

Kemal Bey, lieutenant governor of Yozgat during the massacres there. The reaction to his death reflected the attitude of a large section of Turkish popular opinion. His funeral on 11 April 1919 turned into a public demonstration against the British occupation of Istanbul. Inscriptions on wreaths included 'To the innocent Muslim martyr' and 'Kemal Bey, the Great Martyr of the Turks'.[38] The biggest fish seemed to have escaped altogether. All three members of the ruling Young Turk triumvirate, Talaat, Enver and Djemal, were condemned to death by the Tribunal in their absence. The German navy had whisked them away to safety in Odessa in mid-October 1918, just as the war was drawing to an end. By November of that year Talaat Pasha was in exile in Berlin. There he began to live an unobtrusive life under an assumed name, playing bridge with his cronies, and working on his memoirs.[39]

The political situation in Turkey changed dramatically. The Greek occupation of Smyrna (Izmir) in May 1919 helped to fuel a renewed Turkish nationalism, which found a powerful new leader in Mustafa Kemal. By April 1920 the Kemalist Grand National Assembly had been established in Ankara as an alternative to the Ottoman parliament in Istanbul. A combination of Allied ineptitude and lack of political will meant that promises previously made to the Armenians (including the proposals that were part of the abortive Treaty of Sèvres in 1920) were swiftly forgotten. The newly-established Soviet government awarded the Armenian provinces of Kars and Ardahan to Kemal's resurgent Turkey. America was unwilling to take on a mandate for Western Armenia, and France withdrew from Cilicia, the other area of Turkey which had had a significant Armenian population and heritage.

When the Lausanne Conference reached a final settlement between the Allies and Turkey in July 1923,

Armenia and the Armenians were not even mentioned. The Armenian delegation was only permitted to put its case to a meeting of the Conference's sub-committee on minorities, which was boycotted by Turkey.[40] British diplomats informed an Armenian delegation that had been officially excluded from the Conference that 'the Armenian claims are not a vital issue for the Allies, who are more concerned with the Straits issues'. They added that 'Allies will not sever their relations with Turkey for the sake of the Armenian question'.[41] In a private interview, Sir Horace Rumbold, one of the British representatives, informed Edward Naville and Bonnard Kraft of the International Philarmenian League that:

> We are asked at Lausanne to repair the irreparable. We are not here to impose conditions but to submit to them. The Turks will give way only before force. We have no force to oppose them. It would be unthinkable to recommence the war. We cannot go to war for the Armenians. We recognize all our promises and our engagements, but we are not able to fulfil them. There is nothing to do, we must capitulate, we must conclude peace at any price. Obviously the Armenians are sacrificed.[42]

As time went on a similar pragmatic approach would colour official British attitudes towards recognition of the Armenian Genocide. The Turkey that had been reborn under Atatürk's leadership quickly became a crucial element first in the geopolitics of East and West, and later in the relationship between the West and Islam, as well as emerging as a significant trading partner. Self-interest trumped justice and morality. A memorandum from the Eastern Department of the Foreign and Colonial Office in

1999 revealed that, as Geoffrey Robertson QC has commented, 'this particular genocide could not be recognised – not because it had not taken place, but because it was politically and commercially inconvenient to do so'.[43]

The Allies might have abandoned the Armenians, but the Armenians still managed to pursue some of the guilty men condemned to death by the Ottoman tribunal. Djemal Pasha was assassinated in Tiflis (Tbilisi) in 1922, and in the same year Enver Pasha was killed by a Red Army patrol while trying to stir up a pan-Turkic revolt in Russia. Others implicated in the genocide were also tracked down by Armenian avengers. The most significant assassination of all, however, had come earlier.

At 11am on 15 March 1921, while Talaat Pasha was taking a stroll towards the zoological gardens in Berlin, he was shot dead. The young man responsible was captured by passers-by, and taken to the police station. He had been beaten up by the crowd, some of whom had mistaken his stout victim for General von Kappen, an equally corpulent war hero. They had ignored the murderer's plea, uttered in broken German: 'Me Armenian, him Turkish, no harm for Germany! Let me go, it's nothing to do with you.'

The assassin was a young Turkish Armenian engineering student named Soghomon Tehlirian. He told his interrogators that it was on Talaat's orders that 'my mother, my brother, my sister, my family, my people were massacred', and that he had sworn on his mother's grave that he would kill the former Grand Vizier. He later claimed that he had not known that Talaat was in Berlin until one day he spotted the Turkish politician in the street. Afterwards, in a dream, Tehlirian saw the heap of bodies of his martyred family. His mother's ghost rebuked him for doing nothing while he knew where their murderer was.[44]

Tehlirian's trial shone a spotlight on the sufferings of the

Armenians. Witnesses included the prominent German missionary Dr Johannes Lepsius, General Liman von Sanders (who referred to his own success in stopping the Smyrna deportation), as well as several Armenian victims who were able to give graphic descriptions of the atrocities which they had seen. Important testimony was given by the German-speaking Armenian Apostolic Orthodox Bishop based in Manchester, Grigoris Balakian. He had been one of only a handful of survivors from the arrest and deportation of Constantinople's leading Armenian intellectuals on 24 April 1915. Although the Public Prosecutor demanded a verdict of murder, Tehlirian was acquitted. A German Socialist newspaper compared him with the Swiss hero William Tell.[45]

One of those on whom the Tehlirian trial had a particular impact was a young Polish Jewish law student named Raphael Lemkin. He wrote in his autobiography:

Tehlirian, one of the few survivors of the Armenian massacre, had been saved because the body of his dead mother had fallen over him. His trial became, in actuality, a trial of the Turkish perpetrators. The sinister panorama of the destruction of the Armenians was painted by the many witnesses the Armenians brought to the court. Through this trial the world finally obtained a true picture of the tragic events in Turkey. The same world that was conveniently silent when the Armenians were murdered and had intended to hide the fact by releasing the Turkish war criminals was now compelled to listen to the awful truth.

His reflections on the atrocities committed against the Armenians led him to feel 'that a law against this type of racial or religious murder must be adopted by the world'.

When his professors at Lwow University argued that such a law would interfere with the sovereignty of states, he answered that 'sovereignty ... cannot be conceived as the right to kill millions of innocent people'.[46] Lemkin would go on to coin the word 'genocide' in 1944, persuading the United Nations to adopt the 'Convention for the Prevention and Punishment of Genocide' four years later.

Meanwhile, under Atatürk and his successors, the Turks began to develop a view of their own history from which the Armenians were increasingly erased. Uğur Ümit Üngör, the Turkish-born Dutch historian, notes how 'the Kemalist regime continued on all fronts the preceding Young Turk policies of effacing physical traces of Armenian existence: churches were defaced and buildings rid of their Armenian descriptions'. He adds that 'although the Armenians were gone, in a sense they were still deemed too visible'. During the Genocide a Turkish Commissioner of Deportation had told Rössler, the German Consul in Aleppo, 'We want an Armenia without Armenians.' Now millennia of Armenian history, religion and culture were also to be eliminated.[47]

The impact of this wiping out of a people's past can be almost as devastating as the denial of the Genocide for those who find that their identity is treated as non-existent. The Armenian-American author Herand Markarian, born in Iraq to Genocide survivors, describes a visit to a museum in modern Turkey. His reference to Dikran (Tigran) the Great is to the first century B.C. Armenian ruler who established an empire that stretched from the Caspian Sea to the Mediterranean. Ani was the medieval Armenian capital, once famed as 'the city of a thousand and one churches'. Its ruins are in territory given by Soviet Russia to Turkey:

> We visit the museum of Aintab. Outside in the yard, alongside many Roman tombstones, we find two

inscribed in Armenian; however there is no reference to their origin.

Inside the museum, there is a beautiful display of costumes and designs. On the wall there is a chronological table of historical sites and political powers that reigned in these lands. I look for Armenian names and places. I cannot find them. I look for the names of Dikran the Great and the city of Ani. I cannot find them.

One of the non-Armenian members of our tour group comes closer and looks at the display and comments, *'Where is Ani?'* I look at him and say, *'We have never existed.'* Shaking his head he says, *'Now I understand.'*[48]

[1] Wolfgang Gust (editor), *The Armenian Genocide: Evidence from the German Foreign Office Archives, 1915-1916* (New York: Berghahn Books, 2014), p.738.

[2] Vahakn N. Dadrian, foreword to Gust (ed), *The Armenian Genocide*,p.xviii

[3] Raymond Kévorkian, *The Armenian Genocide: A Complete History* (London: I.B.Tauris, 2011), p.538.

[4] Gust (ed), *The Armenian Genocide*, pp.490-3.

[5] Tacy Atkinson, *'The German, the Turk and the Devil Made a Triple Alliance':
Harpoot Diaries, 1908-1917* (Princeton, New Jersey: Gomidas Institute), p.43.

[6] Bertha B. Morley, *Marsovan 1915: The Diaries of Bertha Morley*, second edition, edited by Hilmar Kaiser (Ann Arbor, Michigan: Gomidas Institute, 2000), p.24.

[7] Gust (ed), *The Armenian Genocide*, pp.466-8.

[8] Vahakn N. Dadrian, *German Responsibility in the Armenian Genocide: A Review of the Historical Evidence of German Complicity* (Watertown, Massachusetts: Blue Crane Books, 1996), p.115.

[9] Gust (ed), *The Armenian Genocide*, p.758.

[10] Henry Morgenthau, *United States Diplomacy on the Bosphorus: The Diaries of Ambassador Morgenthau 1913-1916*, compiled by Ara Sarafian (Princeton, New Jersey: Gomidas Institute, 2004), p.327; Gust, *The Armenian Genocide*, p.395; Hervé Georgelin, 'Inter-Community Relations in Late Ottoman Smyrna' in Richard G. Hovannisian (editor), *Armenian Smyrna/Izmir: The Aegean Communities* (Costa Mesa, California: Mazda Publishers, 2012), p.190.

[11] Gust (ed), *The Armenian Genocide*, pp.678-81; Marjorie Housepian Dobkin, *Smyrna 1922: Destruction of a City* (New York: Newmark Press, 1998).

[12] Vahakn N.Dadrian and Taner Akçam, *Judgment at Istanbul: The Armenian Genocide Trials* (New York: Berghahn Books, 2011) pp.279-80.

[13] Gust (ed), *Armenian Genocide*, pp.230-1.

[14] Henry Morgenthau, *Ambassador Morgenthau's Story: A Personal Account of the Armenian Genocide* (New York: Cosimo Classics, 2008), p.261.

[15] Rafael de Nogales, *Four Years Beneath the Crescent* (London: Sterndale Classics, 2003) p.125.

[16] Ara Sarafian, *Talaat Pasha's Report on the Armenian Genocide* (London: Gomidas Institute, 2011), p.6.

[17] Gust (ed), *The Armenian Genocide*, pp.566-7.

[18] Gust (ed), *The Armenian Genocide*, pp.714-15.

[19] Gust (ed), *The Armenian Genocide*, pp.739-40.

[20] Gust (ed), *The Armenion Genocide*, p.199. Gust prints the complete text of the declaration, issued through Agence Havas.

[21] Dadrian and Akçam, *The Armenian Genocide*, p.17.

[22] Dadrian and Akçam, *Judgment at Istanbul*, pp.143-4. See also p.152, note 36, for details of Dadrian's source.

[23] Morley, *Marsovan 1915*, p.14.

[24] Gust (ed), *Armenian Genocide*, p.376.

[25] Gust (ed),*The Armenian Genocide*, p.752.

[26] Kévorkian, *The Armenian Genocide*, p.704.

[27] Dadrian and Akçam, *Judgment at Istanbul*, pp.47-8.

[28] Gust (ed), *The Armenian Genocide*, p.634.

[29] Dadrian and Akçam, *Judgment at Istanbul,* p.45.

[30] Richard G. Hovannisian, *The Republic of Armenia, Volume II: From Versailles to London, 1919-1920* (Berkeley, California: University of California Press, 1982), p.356.

[31] K.B. Bardakjian, *Hitler and the Armenian Genocide* (Cambridge, Massachusetts: The Zoryan Institute, 1985), p.6.

[32] Yair Auron, *The Armenian Genocide: Forgotten and Denied* (Tel-Aviv: Contento De Semrik, 2013), p.167.

[33] Ara Sarafian and Eric Avebury, *British Parliamentary Debates on the Armenian Genocide* (Princeton, New Jersey: Gomidas Institute, 2003), p.2. For the debate, see House of Lords, Hansard (5th series), Vol. XIX, 28 July 1915, col. 774-78.

[34] Dadrian and Akçam, *Judgment at Istanbul*, p.126.

[35] Kévorkian, *The Armenian Genocide*, p.106.

[36] Dadrian and Akçam, *Judgment at Istanbul*, p.109.

[37] Dadrian and Akçam, *Judgment at Istanbul*, p.195.

[38] Taner Akçam, A Shameful Act: *The Armenian Genocide and the Question of Turkish Responsibility* (New York: Henry Holt and Company, 2006), p.293

[39] Edward Alexander, *Crime of Vengeance: An Armenian Struggle for Justice* (New York: The Free Press, 1991), pp.129-33.

[40] Margery Mangigian Tarzian, *The Armenian Minority Problem 1914-1934: A Nation's Struggle for Security* (Atlanta, Georgia: Scholars Press, 1992), pp.174-6.

[41] Akçam, *A Shameful Act*, p.365.

[42] Tarzian, *The Armenian Minority Problem*, pp.177-8.

[43] Geoffrey Robertson, *Was There an Armenian Genocide? Geoffrey Robertson QC's Opinion* (London: Armenian Legal Initiative UK, 2009), p.25.

[44] Jacques Derogy, *Resistance and Revenge: The Armenian Assassination of the Turkish Leaders Responsible for the 1915 Massacres and Deportations* (New Brunswick, New Jersey, 1990), pp.xix-xxiv.

[45] 'Talaat's Assailant Acquitted', *The Times*, Saturday, June 4, 1921, in *The Times of the Armenian Genocide:Reports in the British Press,Volume 2: 1920-1923*, edited by Katia Minas Peltekian (Beirut: Four Roads, 2013), p.822; Derogy, Resistance and Revenge, p.xxiv.

[46] *Totally Unofficial: The Autobiography of Raphael Lemkin*, edited by Donna-Lee Frieze (New Haven,Connecticut: Yale University Press), p.20.

[47] Uğur Ümit Üngör, *The Making of Modern Turkey: Nation and State in Eastern Anatolia, 1913-1950* (Oxford: Oxford University Press, 2012), p.219; Gust (ed), *Armenian Genocide*, p.69.

2. CAUGHT BETWEEN EMPIRES

THE FIRST CHRISTIAN NATION

Greater Armenia (including those provinces which became part of Ottoman Turkey) had long possessed a crucial strategic significance. The historical geographer Robert Hewsen has pointed out that 'whoever dominated the Armenian plateau prior to the twentieth century dominated the entire Middle East'.[1] The result was that, apart from the brief Armenian Empire of Tigran the Great in the first century B.C., Armenians normally found themselves either crushed between rival great powers or overwhelmed by brutal incursions from outside.

The catalogue of those who conquered Armenia (and sometimes divided it between them) is formidable. Hewsen prints a map that shows the foreign invaders coming from four directions across the centuries over several millennia: Hittites, Macedonians, Romans, Byzantines, Crusaders and Ottoman Turks coming from the west; Cimmerians, Scythians, Alans, Khazars, Georgians, Russians and Soviets appearing from the north across the Caucasus Mountains; Assyrians, Arabs and Egyptian Mamluks attacking from the south-west; and Medes, Persians, Parthians, Seljuk Turks and Mongols attacking from the south-east.[2]

Being a bridge between Asia and Europe has enabled Armenians to develop a rich, distinctive and attractive culture. It has also meant that their history has contained far more than its share of misery and atrocities, culminating in the horror of the Genocide of 1915. Perhaps the event that came closest to that final tragedy was the invasion of Armenia by 'Lank-Tamur' (Tamerlane) in 1387. Two years later a scribe named Karapet copied a book of homilies on the island of Aghtamar in Lake Van. He added a colophon describing some of the atrocities carried out by the Mongols:

The corpses of some floated in a sea of blood; some, whose heads were half cut off from their bodies, pleaded for water and soon died of thirst; [and] fountains of blood gushed out of the mouths of those whose heads were dangling ... Now, the sea of horsemen ... went about in search of the Christians, and when they found them they mercilessly slaughtered them / / / they numbered in thousands. They put the wondrous bishops to the sword; they ground the heads of the pious priests between stones; they cast the flock of Christ as food for the dogs; they trampled the children with their horses; they debauched the women, and carried off their infants into captivity.[3]

Yet despite such cruelty, which has earned Tamerlane a lasting place in Armenian folklore, the Armenians survived – and still survive.

Part of the reason for the astonishing resilience of the Armenian people across the centuries is connected with an innate capacity for survival against the odds. The strength of family relationships may also be significant. An integral element of Armenian identity, however, is the knowledge of being part of the oldest Christian nation. Armenia was the first country to accept Christianity as its state religion when King Trdat was converted by the courageous St Gregory the Illuminator in the year 301. A French commentator notes that the horrific tortures which the holy man underwent before the king's conversion are often seen as a prefiguration of Armenia's destiny.[4]

The link between Armenian identity and the Christian faith was strengthened a century later, when St Mesrop Mashtots devised an alphabet particularly suited to the Armenian language, which enabled him to produce the first Armenian translation of the Bible. In 451, on the plain of Avarayr, St Vardan Mamikonian and his Armenian warriors confronted a numerically superior Persian army, intent on imposing Zoroastrianism on his people. Vardan encouraged his soldiers by telling them that their faith was as indelible as the colour of their skin, and not simply a garment that they could put on or off at will.[5]

Clinging to their Christian faith has often made the lives of the Armenians extremely difficult. At different times they have faced persecution by Zoroastrians, Muslims and Soviet atheists, as well as coming under pressure from other branches of the Christian faith which hoped to dominate and absorb the unique Armenian strand of Christianity. Yet, as Vardapet Karekin Sarkissian (later to become His Holiness Catholicos Karekin I), noted in *A Brief Introduction to Armenian Christian Literature*, the story of Armenian Christianity is not solely one of persecution and martyrdom.[6] There have been glorious periods of creativity, producing a distinctive church architecture that has had a wide-ranging influence, mystical poetry of extraordinary depth and power, illuminated manuscripts which are among the greatest masterpieces of Christian art, and the uniquely Armenian *khatchkars* or cross-stones, whose intricate carvings symbolise the triumph of life over suffering and death through Christ's victory on the Cross.

In Lake Van, in that part of eastern Turkey, which is now 'Armenia without Armenians', there is a remarkable church on the little island of Aghtamar: the place where the scribe Karapet once poured out his grief at the agonies inflicted by Tamerlane. It was built in the second decade of the tenth century for King Gagik, Armenian ruler of Vaspurakan. The Church of the Holy Cross, Aghtamar, is particularly famous for the reliefs and friezes carved on its exterior. Many of them depict Biblical themes, but one shows the monarch presenting a model of the church to Christ (some observers have been unable to resist pointing out that King Gagik appears to be slightly taller than his Lord). These days Aghtamar has been turned into a tourist attraction by the Turkish authorities, and the Armenians are only permitted to celebrate the Liturgy there once a year. Before the Genocide it was a place of frequent pilgrimage.[7]

Among those pre-Genocide pilgrims was a boy named Manoug Adoian, who was born at Khorkom, on the shores of Lake Van. Like many of his compatriots, his life would become a complicated journey. As a fourteen-year-old boy he took part in the defence of Van, where the Armenians were besieged by Turkish forces bent on massacre. The Russians relieved the city, but then retreated. Manoug and his family were among the refugees who made the agonising journey across the mountains. They went to the Armenian spiritual centre of Etchmiadzin, and then on to Yerevan, the capital. Conditions were terrible. The winter months of 1918-1919 were a time of starvation in the newly independent country. A fifth of the population died. As the famine continued into March, Manoug's thirty-nine-year-old mother was among the victims. He left Armenia and travelled via Batum to Constantinople. In February 1920 he embarked on a ship to America.

In the United States the young Armenian would be transformed into the painter Arshile Gorky. Among his best known works is 'The Artist and His Mother', painted between 1926 and 1935, and now in the National Gallery of Art at Washington DC (another version is in the Whitney Museum of Modern Art). Nouritza Matossian, in her biography of the artist, was the first to identify the connection between Arshile Gorky's masterpiece and the island church which he had visited in his childhood:

> No other source or influence captures the essence of his double portrait more vividly than the austere frescoes and stone reliefs of the Virgin and saints in the Church of the Holy Cross at Aghtamar. The strong, rigid figures in hieratic poses with their features simplified into geometric patterns, the severe and hypnotic gaze of the huge dark eyes had caught young Manoug's gaze.

The biographer goes on to analyse the relationship between the painting and the artist's traumatic childhood and adolescence:

> Confident of his expertise at last, he painted in answer to a strong inner need. His homage to his mother was bound to take on a sacred quality. Gorky's experience as a survivor of the Armenian Genocide is at the root of its spiritual power and explains its captivating poignancy. It had been his goal for years. He saved her from oblivion, snatching her at last out of the pile of corpses to place her on a pedestal ...

He painted himself and his mother in shades of the rose tufa of Aghtamar. She is his lost homeland retrieved, the resplendent Armenian earth and stone. Fearful of losing his childhood and his identity, he placed himself next to his mother and painted her back to life.[8]

Even after the Western Armenians had lost their homeland its memory would continue both to haunt and to inspire them.

PROGRESS AND REACTION

Their particular expression of Christianity played a key role in the survival of the Armenians as a distinct entity during the opening centuries of Turkish rule. Religion, rather than ethnicity, was the touchstone of identity within Ottoman society. The non-Muslim subjects of the Empire were divided into separate self-governing *millets* for the Greek Orthodox, the Jews and the Armenian Apostolic Orthodox. Catholic and Protestant *millets* were added in the nineteenth century. The head of the Armenian *millet* in all matters, both religious and secular, was the Patriarch of Constantinople. This put the church at the centre of Armenian life. It also meant that the cosmopolitan city became a magnet for Ottoman Armenians. In the first Ottoman census of 1477 there were over 400 Armenian families in Constantinople. Four hundred years later the Armenians population of the city was between 162,000 and 300,000.[9]

By the late eighteenth century a group of Armenian *amiras* had emerged in the capital: wealthy magnates who were regarded as valuable servants of the Sultan, and who used their power and influence to control the Patriarch and the millet. In the century that followed they often fulfilled important state functions as financiers, large-scale manufacturers and administrators. Several generations of the Armenian Balian family produced some of the finest Ottoman architecture. A middle class of Armenian merchants and entrepreneurs developed, not only in the capital, but also in many other urban centres. Armenians became teachers, doctors, dentists and pharmacists. Armenian artisans played a crucial role in the life of virtually every community. As well as those who kept to traditional roles as potters, blacksmiths, tailors, shoemakers and bakers, some branched out into new fields, such as photography. In the Armenian heartland of eastern Anatolia, Armenian farmers also strove to improve agricultural methods. Their increasing prosperity inevitably made Armenians the subject of suspicion and envy from some other sections of Ottoman society.[10]

Economic progress led to cultural renaissance. During the nineteenth century Western Armenian developed as a literary language in Constantinople (the same process was taking place with Eastern Armenian in Tiflis). Bedros Tourian, who died of tuberculosis aged 21, produced some powerful lyric poetry in his last two years, providing a pattern and an inspiration for his successors. If Tourian gave a voice to the romantic and tragic side of his people, a very different writer expressed the liveliness and humour that are also essential Armenian characteristics. Hagop Baronian was a playwright and satirist who enjoyed making fun of the pomposities and hypocrisies that existed within Constantinople's Armenian society. Inevitably he trod on far too many toes for his life to be a comfortable one.[11]

Social changes also led to a shift in the internal administration of the Armenian community. A constitutional change, agreed by the Sultan in 1863, lessened the dominance of the *amiras* and the Patriarch, giving greater prominence to the middle class and the laity in community affairs. Through these developments, Razmik Panossian notes, 'the idea of citizenship, of individual rights and civic duties, of constitutionalism and reform-based politics, all entered Armenian political consciousness'. However control of the new National Assembly of the *millet* remained firmly centred on the capital: Constantinople had 80 seats out of 140. Over 80% of Ottoman Armenians lived in the provinces, but they had to make do with the remaining 60 seats.[12]

While the Armenians progressed economically and culturally, the Ottoman Empire was in decline. Dubbed the 'Sick Man of Europe', its territory was steadily eroded. It also faced constant interference from the major European powers. In 1862 a crisis erupted in Zeytun, a fiercely independent-minded Armenian mountain community in Cilicia, which had managed to maintain a degree of autonomy. A Turkish army of some 10,000 men was sent to quell the mountaineers. The people of Zeytun resisted courageously. After two assaults had failed, the Turkish forces retreated. A settlement was brokered with the not especially enthusiastic assistance of the Emperor Napoleon III of France.[13]

Abdul Hamid II became Sultan in 1876. The following year Russia declared war on the Ottoman Empire. The Turks were defeated. In the Treaty of San Stefano the Turks agreed to carry out reforms in the Armenian provinces. Britain, however, seeing the treaty as far too favourable to the Russians, insisted that the European powers should meet to revise its terms. They did so at the Congress of Berlin in 1878. The British, led by Lords Beaconsfield (Disraeli) and Salisbury, did a secret deal with the Turks before the Congress met. Britain was to lease the island of

Cyprus in return for promising to help defend Turkey's eastern border against any future Russian attack. The Congress refused to hear the Armenian delegation. They had to make do with the hollow promise that was article 61 of the Berlin treaty:

> The Sublime Porte undertakes to carry out, without further delay, the improvements and reforms demanded by local requirements in the provinces inhabited by Armenians, and to guarantee their security against the Circassians and Kurds.
>
> It will periodically make known the steps taken to this effect to the powers, who will superintend their application.[14]

During the years that followed the position of the Armenians in the six eastern provinces became increasingly desperate. Paper protests from the European powers had no force. The Sultan was only too aware that France, Germany and Britain all had economic interests in the Ottoman Empire, which they did not want to put at risk. In 1891 Abdul Hamid created the *Hamidiye*, a special force of 30,000 Kurds commanded by one of his relatives. The threat to the Armenians was only too clear. Meanwhile between 1885 and 1890 three Armenian political parties were founded, heavily influenced by European radical, revolutionary and nationalist movements. They were carefully monitored by the Sultan's spies.

Sasun, in the Taurus Mountains, is famed for its connection with the Armenian national epic, *David of Sasun*, which describes the exploits of a dynasty of heroic warriors. In 1894 the Sasun Armenians, already over-burdened with Ottoman state taxes and payments to Muslim landowners, refused to pay an additional levy demanded by the Kurdish chieftains of the area. Turkish soldiers, with the backing of the *Hamidiye*, attacked Sasun. The Armenians defended themselves courageously but were eventually overwhelmed. Several thousand men, women and children were massacred.

Frustrated by the lack of an effective response to the events in Sasun, the Hunchaks (one of the Armenian political parties) arranged the 'Kum Kapu' demonstration in Constantinople on 30 September 1895, intending to deliver a formal protest to the Ottoman government. The major commanding the police attempted to halt the demonstrators. Drawing his sword he struck an Armenian student. The student responded by fatally shooting him. This triggered massacres of Armenians throughout the capital, which were brought to an end by the intervention of the European embassies. They were not, however, able to prevent an explosion of slaughter in the Armenian provinces. It began on 8 October 1895 in Trebizond and eventually claimed between 100,000 and 200,000 victims.

One of the eyewitnesses of the Trebizond massacre, an American missionary, noted that the aim of those involved in the slaughter was to hunt down and kill the men, stripping and mutilating their bodies, which would be buried in trenches or thrown in the sea. The women and children, however, would be left unharmed, unless hurt by accident. The Armenian shops were plundered, and anything of value removed.[15] One of the most appalling events took in Urfa, where 3,000 Armenians (including, in this case, women and children) were burned alive in the Cathedral – which should have been respected as a place of refuge under Islamic law. In March 1896, visiting this scene of horror, a British diplomat commented that, 'even today, two months and a half after the massacre, the smell of putrescent and charred remains is unbearable'. Only the fierce Armenian warriors of

Zeytun successfully resisted for a second time, and even staged a counter-attack.[16]

Arman Kirakossian has commented on the degree of organization and premeditation involved in the Hamidian atrocities:

> In 1895 and 1896 the massacres started almost simultaneously in all provinces. A rifle shot or trumpet sounds from the Muslim quarter of cities would usually signal the beginning of the pogrom. The pogroms of the cities were usually preceded by the savage attacks on the Armenian-populated villages by the Kurdish cavalry. Mobs of Kurds, Circassians, and Lases would storm the cities and, together with the local Turkish population, troops and gendarmes would conduct a massacre of the Armenian population and loot their property. The local authorities were instructed to kill the male population primarily. The only victims of the pogroms were Armenians: the Greeks and Jews were almost unaffected. The massacres of the Armenians were organized, and regular troops and gendarmes took part in murder and looting. The pogroms would end as suddenly as they started, usually after a horn signal.[17]

Robert Hewsen observes that 'the culpability of the Turkish authorities seems beyond question, so much so that Shaw in his pro-Turkish history of the Ottoman Empire makes no mention of the massacres of that year [1895], preferring to ignore them rather than deal with the questions they might arouse'.[18]

On 26 August 1896 a group from the Dashnaks or Armenian Revolutionary Federation, another Armenian political party, seized the Imperial Ottoman Bank in Constantinople. They were led by Babken Siuni, a youth of seventeen. Several of the Dashnaks, including Siuni, were killed while securing the building. The intruders took many of the bank staff as hostages, but the director, Sir Edgar Vincent, managed to escape through a skylight. After negotiating with the government via a Russian diplomatic go-between, the Dashnaks were allowed to leave the Bank and were put on board Sir Edgar's yacht. From there they were transferred to the steamer *Gironde*, which took them to freedom in France.

The Ottoman authorities apparently had prior knowledge of this escapade, but allowed it to go ahead. Revenge was swiftly taken on the Armenians of Constantinople. About 6,000 of them were massacred in an orgy of killing that only stopped when British marines were landed. In two districts the Armenian population was wiped out almost completely. Most of the victims were poor migrant workers who had come to the capital from the provinces in search of security and a better life. The morale of Constantinople's Armenians was shaken by the butchery. In the months that followed some 75,000 of them emigrated abroad.[19]

Among those who were appalled by the massacres of Armenians was the former British Prime Minister, William Ewart Gladstone. In September 1896, aged 86, he came out of retirement to make one last great speech. Addressing a public meeting in Liverpool, he eloquently and angrily condemned the atrocities that had taken place in Turkey. The Armenian merchants of Manchester were so grateful that they gave a silver chalice and a stained glass window to the church where Gladstone worshipped in Hawarden, and Tiflis Armenians presented him with an illuminated Armenian Gospel-book. In a debate in the House of Commons in November 1918, Major Peel reminisced about a visit that he had paid to the ex-Prime Minister towards the end of Gladstone's life:

I came to see the great statesman on another subject, but found that he was entirely absorbed in the thought of Armenia. He told me that just as when a young man his interests had been absorbed in the freedom of Italy so in his old age he felt the first obligation upon him was toward the martyred people of Armenia. He added a phrase which I think I can repeat, 'That of all the nations of the world no history has been so blameless as the history of the Armenian people.'[20]

The Armenian Dilemma

In July 1908 a revolution took place in Turkey. It was led by the 'Young Turks', a group of army officers from Macedonia sympathetic to the opposition Committee of Union and Progress (CUP). On the day after the restoration of the 1876 Constitution was proclaimed in centres throughout European Turkey, Sultan Abdul Hamid had to bow to the inevitable and do the same in Constantinople. The resultant euphoria was probably felt more strongly by the Armenians than by any other section of Ottoman society. Khachadour Maloumian (Agnouni), a leading Dashnak activist, wrote from 'a free Constantinople':

> You can't imagine how happy I am to write to you from this city without fear of being spied on.
> A city where mouths that have been silenced for 32 years together cry 'freedom.' The masses are intoxicated with emotion. After 30 years of silence, it is possible to yell and get drunk for 30 days.[21]

When elections were held later in the year, ten Armenian deputies were elected to the new Parliament: five Dashnaks, two CUP members, one Hunchak, one Liberal and two independents. The most distinguished and respected was the Liberal law professor and short story writer Krikor Zohrab. He would later be a victim of the 1915 Genocide.

If one of the revolutionary aims had been to preserve and strengthen the Ottoman Empire, it soon became clear that this was a hopeless cause. The Austro-Hungarians took advantage of the upheaval, annexing Bosnia and Herzegovina on 5 October 1908. On the same day Bulgaria declared its independence and left the Ottoman Empire. The next day the island of Crete followed its example (it would later become united with Greece). The revolution had not altered the Empire's international position. It continued to disintegrate.

Simmering discontent flared up into counter-revolution on the evening of 13 April 1909. Mutinous soldiers overpowered their officers and marched on Parliament. They were joined by religious students linked to the recently formed Society for Muslim Unity. On the following day the government imploded. The grand vizier resigned and the CUP leaders hastily left Constantinople. After a fortnight of chaos, order was restored by an 'Action Army', formed in Macedonia. The Constitution was re-established and the CUP was returned to power. Sultan Abdul Hamid, the moving force behind the counter-revolution, was deposed in favour of his brother.

This temporary crisis had disastrous results for the Armenians of Cilicia. Adana and the surrounding area became the scene of atrocities that took the lives of some 25,000 people. It was an area that had been untouched by the massacres of 1894-6. The Armenians were prosperous and, thanks to the revolution, now enjoyed political equality. This seems to have bred resentment among some of their Muslim neighbours. Cilicia had been the home of the last independent Armenian kingdom, which was snuffed out in 1375. The authorities had a deep-seated suspicion that the Armenians might rise up and try to reclaim their freedom. Rumours and provocations were rife. It only needed a single incident to spark a conflagration.

This occurred on 9 April 1909. A newly married Armenian carpenter's son, Hovhannes, had been bullied, threatened and beaten by a gang of Turkish thugs. His protest to the governor was ignored. Terrified, the young man bought a pistol to defend himself. The gang, aware that the authorities were unwilling to protect the Armenian, attacked him again. Hovhannes, wounded by their daggers and in fear for his life, drew his pistol and fired at his assailants. He killed the ringleader, mortally wounded a second man, and shot the third in the arm. Then he disappeared. An angry Turkish mob ransacked Hovhannes' family home, beating up his parents and his wife. Tensions grew. The authorities demanded that the Armenians hand over the murderer. They were unable to do so, as they did not know where he was.[22]

Among those stirring up anti-Armenian feeling in Adana, one of the most vocal was Ihsan Fikri, the president of the Adana CUP and director of its local newspaper. On the evening of 9 April Fikri and his fellow Young Turks held a meeting to denounce the *ghiaours* (infidels). Four days later he addressed his fellow Turks, inciting them to act against the Armenians.[23] Apparently the alliance between the CUP and the Armenians as fellow constitutionalists did not reach as far as Adana. A false rumour that Armenians had killed two Turks was followed by another that they had killed two Turkish men and two Turkish women. The governor and other leading figures came together on the night of 13 April and decided that the Armenians deserved to be punished. The local mufti delivered his opinion that massacring

Christians was in accordance with Islamic law. The following day the slaughter began.[24]

In his study of 'The Cilician Massacres', Raymond Kévorkian expresses his certainty that the events in Adana were pre-arranged. The Armenians were attacked by thousands of Kurds, Turks and immigrants from Crete, backed by some of the most important people in the town. After the initial shock they began to defend themselves and held out for three days. Then Osman Bey, a leading Turk who was friendly towards the Armenians, brokered a ceasefire. When Hagop Terzian, the Armenian pharmacist, ventured out to look for medicines and palliatives to help the wounded, he saw that 'the streets were full of corpses, innumerable Armenians either half-dead or deceased'.[25]

The Armenians of Adana had been able to defend themselves because, under the Constitution, they were allowed to bear arms. Now, as the ceasefire entered its second day, they heard that the government wanted them to hand over their weapons. Naturally, they were reluctant to do so. However, the church authorities, both in Constantinople and locally, urged that they comply. Major Doughty-Wylie, the British Consul from nearby Mersin, added his voice to the chorus. 'I can promise you, in the name of my government, that nothing further will happen,' he proclaimed. 'Surrender your weapons.'[26] The Armenians were caught in the same dilemma that they would face in many places after the outbreak of the First World War. If they held on to their weapons for self-defence they would be declared to be dangerously disloyal rebels. If they gave them up they would be left completely defenceless – and would still be likely to be denounced as dangerously disloyal rebels for having had the weapons in the first place.

Trusting in the British Consul's promise (which proved to be an empty one), the Armenians surrendered all their weapons. It was a disastrous decision. As Hagop Terzian noted:

> Had we not handed them over before the arrival of the Ottoman Army, there is no doubt that there would not have been a second massacre, because, despite our lack of military stores, the enemy was very suspicious and had great fears about our strength. Thanks to this imprudent act the second massacre, which was a hundred times worse than the first, took place and destroyed Adana.[27]

During the lull between the two massacres Turkish officials and propagandists attempted to shift all the blame for the events onto the Armenians. The local CUP produced a special issue of its newspaper, *Ittidal* (Moderate), which was distributed free of charge to the Muslim population. Ismail Sefa, the editor, accused the Armenians of having armed themselves from sinister motives: 'they shamelessly launched threats of this kind: one day or another, we will massacre Turks; henceforth we are not afraid'. Adil Bey of the Ministry of the Interior gave an equally misleading report: 'Armenians are the ones who have attacked; they are armed and massacre defenceless Turks ...'[28]

The second Adana massacre began on Sunday 25 April. The unarmed Armenians crowded into churches and religious schools in a vain hope that these might not be attacked. Terzian described the scene in the Armenian church of Sourp Stepanos, where he took refuge for a time:

> ... the mob outside drenched the church dome with *petroleum instead of water* from water pumps and then it set fire to the Armenian Apostolic prelacy with one or two Mauser bullets.
>
> It also became impossible to go into the church

courtyard because it was the church's turn to be attacked. The church began to get very hot and fill with smoke. Despite being totally stone-built, the intense heat made the dome, walls and pillars crack. The people inside, bereft of hope, began to shout in unison, 'Help, help! Have pity on us, we're burning!'

The women, with bloody tears, shouted, *'Der voghormya,'* ['Lord have mercy'] the men called for silence, and the children were asphyxiated; there was shouting and wailing and terrific commotion as the church of Sourp Stepanos became a veritable hell.[29]

Ferriman Duckett noted that the worst atrocities in this second massacre included the burning of a school containing 2,000 sick and wounded people, and the setting on fire of two other hospitals. He reported that Major and Mrs Doughty-Wylie bravely led a 'homeless and haggard' group of Armenians to safety, thus partly compensating for the catastrophic results of the British Consul's empty promise that his government would protect them. The slaughter ended on 27 April, coinciding with the defeat of the counter-revolution in Constantinople and the deposition of Sultan Abdul Hamid.[30]

Two important Armenian writers produced reflections on the killings. One was Zabel Yesayan (Essayan), who would escape the round up of Armenian intellectuals in Constantinople in 1915, only to perish later in the Stalinist purges. She went to Adana in June 1909 as part of an Armenian Red Cross mission sent by the Patriarch to help the victims and arrange care for the orphans. The harrowing reality that she found there led her to write *In the Ruins*, a work which some consider to be her masterpiece.[31] The poet Siamanto received a detailed description of the atrocities and their impact on those caught up in them from a close friend, Dr Diran Balakian, a physician in Adana. As a result he wrote a powerful, angry and disturbing cycle of poems: *Bloody News From My Friend*.

One of them, 'The Dance', is based on an eyewitness account by a German nurse, who had been caring for a dying Armenian woman stabbed in the massacre. Looking out of her window, she saw twenty young Armenian brides, stripped, whipped and forced to dance by a crowd who sang obscene songs and shouted filthy insults at them. The poem (in a translation by Nevart Yaghlian and Dr Dikran's grandson, Peter Balakian) ends:

> Then someone brought a jug of kerosene.
> Human justice, I spit in your face.
> The brides were anointed.
> 'Dance,' they thundered –
> 'here's a fragrance you can't get in Arabia.
>
> With a torch, they set
> the naked brides on fire.
> And the charred bodies rolled
> and tumbled to their deaths ...
>
> I slammed my shutters,
> sat down next to my dead girl
> and asked: 'How can I dig out my eyes?'[32]

Siamanto would be one of several leading Armenian writers to perish in the 1915 Genocide.

The pogroms left a legacy of unease and suspicion. As Kaligian notes, 'official equality as Ottoman subjects had not prevented the murder of Armenians'.[33] It had become clear that, although the followers of Abdul Hamid had played a part in the slaughter, some of the Young Turks were also implicated. The CUP included both progressives and chauvinist nationalists. As the Ottoman Empire continued to be eroded the latter element would become increasingly predominant. With European Turkey slipping away, leaving a legacy of hundreds of thousands of refugees who needed to be resettled, the 'Turkification' of Anatolia, including Western Armenia, became an increasingly important project for many CUP leaders.

A war with Italy from 1911 to 1912 led to the loss of Libya and the Dodecanese. More significantly, Albania and Macedonia ceased to be part of the Ottoman Empire after the disastrous First Balkan War of 1912 to 1913, though the Turks managed to regain the part of eastern Thrace around Edirne (Adrianople) in the Second Balkan War of 1913. Many of the leaders of the CUP had been born in the Balkan lands which the Turks had occupied for four hundred years. Uğur Ümit Üngör has tellingly described the impact that the aftermath of the Balkan Wars had on them:

> The emotions of Young Turk elites expelled from their ancestral lands included humiliation, helplessness, anger, loss of dignity, lack of self-confidence, anxiety, embarrassment, shame: a toxic mix that combined together, contributed to the growth of collective hate and destructive fantasies. ... the loss of power and prestige shattered the conventional myth of an Ottoman identity and Islamic superiority.[34]

Anarchic conditions in the eastern provinces led to pressure on the European embassies in Constantinople to provide protection for the Armenians in their heartland. After a great deal of wrangling, the six powers (Russia, Great Britain, France, Germany, Italy and Austria-Hungary) came to an agreement. The Ottoman government accepted it, extremely unwillingly, in a Reform Act of 8 February 1914. There would be two Armenian provinces, one uniting Trebizond, Sivas and Erzerum, and the other composed of Van, Bitlis, Kharpert and Diarbekir. Each would come under a foreign inspector-general. Major Nicolai Hoff from the Norwegian ministry of war and Louis Westenenk, a former Dutch colonial administrator, were appointed to these posts. In the summer of 1918 Hoff reached Van, while Westenenk was still on his way via Constantinople.[35]

The Armenians were hopeful about the new arrangements. The CUP leaders were furious. They feared that Western Armenia under foreign oversight was in danger of breaking away as the Ottoman Empire's former possessions in the Balkans had done. They also resented the way in which the European powers were once again using the troubles of the Armenians as an excuse for intervening in Turkish internal affairs. One answer might be to get rid of this irritating minority altogether. As a World War came closer the seeds of genocide began to germinate.

---

[1] Robert H. Hewsen, *Armenia: A Historical Atlas* (Chicago: University of Chicago Press, 2001), p.9.

[2] Hewsen, *Armenia*, p.15.

[3] Avedis K. Sanjian, *Colophons of Armenian Manuscripts, 1301-1480: A Source for Middle Eastern History* (Cambridge, Massachusetts: Harvard University Press, 1969), p.108.

[4] Luc-André Marcel, *Grégoire de Narek et l'ancienne poésie arménienne* (Yerevan: Nahapet, 2005), p.4.

[5] Robert W. Thomson, *Ełishē: History of Vardan and the Armenian War* (Cambridge, Massachusetts: Harvard University Press, 1982), pp.154-5.

[6] Vardapet Karekin Sarkissian, *A Brief Introduction to Armenian Christian Literature* (London: The Faith Press, 1960), pp.10-11.

[7] A beautifully illustrated introduction to the Church of the Holy Cross is Step'an Mnats'akanian, *Aghtamar* (Yerevan: Editions Erebouni, 1986). This has now been republished and reformatted in an attractive bilingual English and Turkish edition: Ara Sarafian and Osman Köker (compilers), *Aghtamar: A Jewel of Medieval Armenian Architecture* (London and Istanbul: Gomidas Institute and Birzamanlar Yayincilik, 2010).

[8] Nouritza Matossian, *Black Angel: A Life of Arshile Gorky* (London: Chatto & Windus, 1998), pp.215, 217-18.

[9] Razmik Panossian, *The Armenians: From Kings and Priests to Merchants and Commissars* (London: Hurst & Company, 2006), pp.69-72; Ronald T. Marchese and Marlene R. Breu, 'Intersection of Society, Culture and Religion: The Constantinople Style and Armenian Identity' in Richard G. Hovannisian and Simon Payaslian (editors), *Armenian Constantinople* (Costa Mesa, California: Mazda Publishers, 2010), pp.103, 112.

[10] Panossian, *The Armenians*, pp.85-6; Maxime K. Yevadian (editor), *Des serviteurs fidèles: Les enfants d'Arménie au service de l'État turc* (Lyons: Sources d'Arménie, 2010), pp.113-4;127-38.

[11] For English translations see James R. Russell, *Bosphorus Nights: The Complete Lyric Poems of Bedros Tourian* (Cambridge, Massachusetts: Harvard University Press, 2005); Hagop Baronian, *Uncle Balthazar: A Comedy in Three Acts* (Boston, Massachusetts: Van Press, 1933); Hagop Baronian, *Honourable Beggars* (London: Mashtots Press, 1978); Hagop Baronian, *The Perils of Politeness* (New York: Ashod Press, 1983).

[12] Panossian, *The Armenians*, pp.148-53.

[13] Christopher J. Walker, *Armenia: The Survival of a Nation* (London: Croom Helm, 1980), pp.100-2.

[14] Walker, *Armenia*, p.115.

[15] Barbara J. Merguerian, 'Reform, Revolution and Repression: The Trebizond Armenians in the 1890s' in Richard G. Hovannisian (editor), *Armenian Pontus: The Trebizond-Black Sea Communities* (Costa Mesa Publishers, California, 2009), p.259-60.

[16] Walker, *Armenia*, pp.161-4.

[17] Arman J. Kirakossion (editor), *The Armenian Massacres 1894-1896: US Media Testimony* (Detroit: Wayne State University Press, 2004), p.29.

[18] Hewsen, *Armenia*, p.231.

[19] Walker, *Armenia*, pp.164-8.

[20] Sarafian and Avebury, *British Parliamentary Debates*, p.45.

[21] Dikran Mesrob Kaligian, *Armenian Organization and Ideology under Ottoman Rule 1908-1914* (New Brunswick, New Jersey: Transaction Publishers, 2009), p.14.

[22] Hagop H. Terzian, *Cilicia 1909: The Massacre of Armenians*, edited by Ara Sarafian (London: Gomidas Institute, 2009), pp.8-10.

[23] Ferriman Duckett, *Turkish Atrocities: The Young Turks and the Truth about the Holocaust at Adana in Asia Minor, during April, 1909 – Written and compiled in April, 1911* (Yerevan: The Armenian Genocide Museum-Institute, 2009), p.16.

[24] Raymond H. Kévorkian, 'The Cilician Massacres, April 1919' in Richard G. Hovannisian and Simon Payaslian (editors), *Armenian Cilicia* (Costa Mesa, California: Mazda Publishers, 2008), pp.341-2.

[25] Kévorkian, 'The Cilician Massacres', p.342; Terzian, *Cilicia 1909*, pp.31-2.

[26] Terzian, *Cilicia 1909*, p.35.

[27] Terzian, *Cilicia 1909*, pp.35-6.

[28] Kévorkian, 'The Cilician Massacres', pp.348-50.

[29] Terzian, *Cilicia 1909*, p.43.

[30] Duckett, *Turkish Atrocities*, pp.23-4.

[31] It has not yet appeared in English, but a French translation by Léon Ketcheyan is available: Zabel Essayan, *Dans les ruines* (Paris: Phébus, 2011).

[32] *Bloody News From My Friend: Poems by Siamanto*, translated by Peter Balakian and Nevart Yaghlian (Detroit: Wayne State University Press, 1996), pp.41-3.

[33] Kaligian, *Armenian Organization*, p.37.

[34] Üngör, *The Making of Modern Turkey*, p.46.

[35] Richard G. Hovannisian (editor), *Armenian People from Ancient to Modern Times, Volume II: Foreign Domination to Statehood: The Fifteenth Century to the Twentieth Century*, second edition (New York: St. Martin's Press), pp.235-8.

3. COMMENCING GENOCIDE

PARANOIA AND PREPARATION

As the summer of 1914 continued, and war between the Ottoman Empire and Russia became increasingly inevitable, the Armenians were faced with an appalling dilemma. They had substantial populations on both sides of the border. The Young Turks attempted to take advantage of this. They approached the Dashnak (Armenian Revolutionary Federation) leaders in the hope that they would persuade the Eastern Armenians to pretend support for their Russian overlords, and then act against them at a crucial moment to assist a Turkish invasion of the Caucasus. Should they be willing to do so, Armenia would be given a degree of autonomy as a reward.

Although relationships between the Russian Armenians and their government had at times been tense and difficult (particularly during a period of attempted 'Russification'), past history had also taught Armenians to be wary of Turkish promises. The Dashnaks therefore informed the

CUP negotiators that Ottoman and Russian Armenians would loyally serve and fight for the empires of which they were citizens. Not all Armenians accepted this policy. The Hunchak party was committed to oppose the Ottoman Empire, and several of their leading members would later be hanged as a result.

Young Turk paranoia about potential Armenian disloyalty was fuelled by the news that the high profile Dashnak parliamentary deputy for Erzerum, Armen Garo (Karekin Pastermadjian), had slipped over the border to join an Armenian partisan unit in Russia. Christopher Walker has commented that his 'action was foolish and short-sighted, and shows that Pastermadjian cannot have appreciated the delicacy of the Armenian position'. Zaven Der Yeghiayan, the Armenian Patriarch of Constantinople from 1913 to 1922, was of the same opinion. He regarded the deputy's behaviour as 'exposing his own party and Turkish-Armenians in general to accusations'. The Ottoman government would exploit the example of Armen Garo in their response to Allied criticism of their anti-Armenian activities.[1]

One result of the 1908 revolution was that Armenians were as eligible as other Ottoman citizens for conscription to the armed forces. Although war would not be declared until the end of October 1914, mobilization began on 2-3 August. Male Armenians were divided into three groups; those between 20 and 45, those between 15 and 20, and those between 45 and 60. The third group was used to carry heavy loads for military purposes.[2] Some Armenian men were able to purchase exemption from conscription, but the result of the mobilization was that Armenian communities were deprived of most of their young and middle-aged men. Sokrat Hakey Mkrtichian, a genocide survivor from the Bitlis region, who was thirteen years old in 1914, described the fate of the older men who were used as beasts of burden:

> Under the severe winter conditions of the Armenian
> Highland, they loaded elderly men from Bitlis, Van,
> Erzroom, Kharbert, Sebastia and other places with 3 – 4
> poods of barley to carry to Sarighamish for the Turkish
> army. That was the most cruel, the meanest, the most
> malicious, brutal and disgusting plan, which started in
> 1914 to annihilate the Armenian males, silently under
> the effect of cold and hunger. From the very beginning of
> World War I the snow-covered roads were covered with
> the corpses of Armenian men. They took away my father
> as well, and we never saw him again.[3]

There was another development that would prove fateful for
the Armenians. This was the creation of an internal branch
of the 'Special Organization', an irregular militia which was
originally intended to operate behind enemy lines in Russia
and Iran. The new units were recruited from three sources:
Kurdish tribes, criminals (particularly those with a
reputation as brigands and gang leaders), and Muslim
refugees from Rumelia (the former European Turkish
provinces) and the Caucasus. They came under the
command either of army officers or of the local secretaries of
the CUP, while the head of the Organization was Dr
Bahaeddin Shakir.

At least ten thousand convicts, the majority of whom
had been sentenced for committing murders, were released
to become part of the Special Organization. The result was
the creation of killing squads who would play a key role
when the full fury of genocide was unleashed on the
Armenians in 1915. The total number of those involved may
have been as many as thirty thousand.[4] Dr Frederick
MacCallum, an American missionary, came across

hundreds of these men, 'dressed in a peculiar uniform', being drilled in Constantinople. He was told that 'they were criminals condemned to penal servitude for life, but had been released from the prisons and given a certain amount of military training and then sent to take charge of the Armenians, who were being deported from various centres in Asia Minor.'[5]

In his diary, Vahram Dadrian gives a thumb-nail sketch of a typical Special Organization recruit. Yusuf was a bandit leader who had been active in the mountains above Dadrian's home town of Chorum for many years. The authorities had failed to capture him, and had put a price of £100 on his head, in the hope that someone else might succeed in doing so. Yusuf, however, had now been pardoned on condition that he joined the irregular troops of the Special Organization. Having heard the news, he came down from his secret lair to Chorum and the governor received him with honour. All the life prisoners were set free a few days later: 'under Yusuf's command, all these murderers formed an army of assassins'.[6]

Once hostilities had been declared, Enver Pasha, the Minister of War and member of the ruling triumvirate, had decided on an audacious attack on the Caucasus front. The career of his hero and role model, the Emperor Napoleon, might perhaps have suggested to him that attacking Russia in the depths of winter was unwise, but Enver does not seem to have taken this into account. Maria Jacobsen, a Danish missionary at Kharpert (Harpoot), was more perceptive. 'And the poor soldiers,' she wrote in her diary, 'what will they have to suffer and endure on their march to the coast and to the Russian border, without food, bedding, or clothes at this cold time with heavy rain? Most of them will die, or suffer for the rest of their lives.'[7]

Enver Pasha had no such concerns. He was hoping for a

dramatic victory. Instead the Turkish army suffered a devastating defeat in the snows of Sarikamish. Two leading military historians of warfare in the Caucasus pay tribute to the courage of the ill-equipped Turkish soldiers, commenting that Sarikamish 'must live in history as the most heroic manifestation of the spirit of the Turkish fighting man'. However the Turkish Third Army had lost 75,000 men and most of its artillery in the offensive. In mid-January 1915 only 18,000 were left.[8] On his way back to Constantinople, the Turkish triumvir gave two Armenian bishops letters praising the loyalty of the Ottoman Armenian troops. An Armenian Sergeant Major named Hovhannes had been personally responsible for preventing Enver Pasha from falling into enemy hands. He was promoted to Captain on the spot, so Enver told the Armenian Patriarch. Patriarch Zaven would later ask himself: 'Did the poor man Hovhannes know that he had just saved his Nation's executioner, and perhaps his own?'[9]

Defeats require a scapegoat and, however valiant and loyal they might have been on the battlefield, the Armenian soldiers remained the obvious candidate. Enver began to accuse the Armenians of treachery, blaming them for the defeat. On 25 February 1915 he sent out an order that all Armenian soldiers in Ottoman army units were to be disarmed. They were then formed into labour battalions.[10] Tacy Atkinson, one of the American missionaries in Kharpert, noticed a growing fearfulness among the Armenian soldiers who were hospital patients in the spring of 1915. One delirious man kept on repeating 'Count the Armenians, count the Armenians.' He later committed suicide.[11]

Verjiné Svazlian has collected two songs about these disarmed soldiers. The first is sung by one of the men:

Mother, mother! I was called up and taken away,
I wasn't given a rifle, but was enlisted in the labour
    battalion.
The Tokat village of Yatmish was less than four days
    distant,
The stones of Yatmish had to be broken down;
The waters of Tokat were so abundant,
Everybody's hope was to come back,
Days, days, I go in such grievous days,
I go, I go, I go as a soldier,
I go to break stones.

The other song is a lament by someone who knows the fate
of many of the men of the Armenian labour battalions:

They took the soldiers to Balou,
Mothers and sisters sat down and wept,
There they made the soldiers dig many pits
And then they buried the soldiers in those pits![12]

Dr Clarence Ussher, the American missionary physician at
Van, described what happened to these tragic conscripts:

The disarmed soldiers, among whom were men of
education and refinement, some of them graduates of
noted American and English universities, were set to
digging trenches and making roads. When the makers of
roads had finished their work, their Turkish officers, first
circulating a report that they were in revolt, had groups
of them surrounded and shot down. This action was not
confined to the province of Van; it was so general as to
make one more than suspect secret orders from
Constantinople.[13]

There is evidence that the slaughter of Armenian labourers started even before Enver's edict that disarmed the soldiers. Early in February 1915 Hayg Toroyan, an Armenian living at Jerablus on the banks of the Euphrates saw 'a column of emaciated, half-dead, terrified, almost naked Armenian workers'. They were the survivors of a group of two thousand Armenian labourers working on the construction of the Baghdad Railway. Their camp had been surrounded by Chechens and Circassians who had stripped them and taken them away to be slaughtered. While this butchery was under way, their horrified surveyors and foremen had persuaded the local district governor to intervene, thus saving some of the men. The commanding officer of the killers showed the governor the telegram ordering him to massacre his victims.[14]

Members of conscript labour battalions were sometimes killed in small groups. Robert Stapleton, a missionary in Erzerum, contacted the American Consul in Tiflis in 1916, describing the shooting of fifty of them in Erzincan. His informant was one of the four men who had managed to escape by falling down and hiding under the corpses of their comrades.[15] Often the slaughter was on a larger scale. Venezuela's contribution to the Ottoman army, the mercenary officer Rafael de Nogales, made a horrifying discovery on the way from Aleppo to Diarbekir. He noticed some gleaming black bundles among the dry reed beds, and went to examine them. They turned out to be 'nothing less than the swollen and worm-eaten corpses of dozens and perhaps hundreds of Armenian soldiers, whom the escort had evidently led from the road and knifed without mercy'.

Later in the day Nogales came across 'thirteen or fifteen hundred unarmed Armenian soldiers breaking stone and mending road'. He refers to 'their furtive frightened glances'. They were presumably aware of what would almost certainly be done to them once their task was completed.[16] Disarmed Armenian conscripts were sometimes massacred in huge numbers. 5,000 were slaughtered and buried in mass graves near Erzincan. A similar number were killed in the Sansar gorge east of Erzerum. A deportee who had managed to escape and was trying to reach safety in the Kurdish haven of Dersim, came across the bodies of 4,000 Armenian soldier labourers from Kharpert who had been working on a road near Palu (perhaps the one mentioned in the lament that Svazlian collected).[17]

An additional tragedy was the fate of the Armenian soldiers' wives and families. In a report to American Ambassador Morgenthau in September 1915, Dr William S. Dodd included a description of the bureaucratic nightmare which these wives faced in when trying to assert their legal right to be excluded from the convoys of deportees:

Soldiers' families are also said to be exempt from deportation, but in countless cases they are swept away with the rest. The wife must put in a special petition claiming her relationship. This petition has to be paid for, for she cannot write Osmanly. It must be stamped with the regular stamp, the additional stamp, the Hedjaz railway stamp and the War-aid stamp. Then after the usual delays of 'go and come again,' a telegram is written to the army post where she says the soldier is, and this she must pay for, thirty to sixty piastres. And all this when she and the children are hungry for bread and no money to buy it. A woman came for treatment yesterday with three children two almost dying. She happened to mention that she was a soldier's wife. I asked her why she did not get free by that. 'They wanted thirty-one piastres for the telegram and I had nothing' was her reply.[18]

On 15 September 1916 Consul Rössler from Aleppo sent the German Chargé d'Affaires in Constantinople a statistical report compiled by Sister Beatrice Rohner, giving details of the Armenian orphans in her care. Out of 720 children, 246 were listed as offspring of 'mothers who were deported while their husbands served in the army'.[19]

The conscription of the men of military age deprived the Armenian communities of most of those who might otherwise have protected those who were left behind: the women, the elderly and the children. The disarming of these conscripts took the process a stage further. It was a visible sign that, as far as the Turkish authorities were concerned, the Armenians were both unreliable and expendable. The soldier labourers were either worked to death or deliberately slaughtered. This was an important element of the developing pattern of genocide. Yet Enver Pasha, the embittered general responsible for the slaughter, was also the man who owed his life to Sergeant Major Yovhannes, the courageous and loyal Ottoman Armenian. As Patriarch Zaven realized, the savage irony was almost beyond words.

ZEYTUN AND VAN

For several months malicious rumours had been spread portraying the Armenians as traitors who would rise up and massacre their Turkish neighbours at the first opportunity. In this hostile atmosphere a single incident would suffice to trigger the plans which the Young Turk leaders had developed to eliminate the Armenians altogether.

Zeytun was an obvious potential flashpoint. Its hardy mountain fighters had a long tradition of independence and successful resistance to government oppression. An Armenian employee of the German consulate in Adana stressed the unwillingness of Zeytun's inhabitants to enlist in the army, and the tendency of those who were conscripted to desert. Nazareth Tchavoush, described as by Toroyan as 'a popular hero', but by the German Consul in Aleppo as 'head of those deserters who were roaming the mountains for months and who became, in time, a brigand chieftain' was captured by the Turks through trickery, imprisoned and beaten to death in his cell.[20]

Pierre Briquet from Tarsus reported on 14 March 1915 how the Turkish gendarmes in Zeytun had been 'molesting the inhabitants, raiding shops, stealing, maltreating the people and dishonouring their women'. He commented that 'it is obvious that the Government are trying to get a case against the Zeitounlis, so as to be able to exterminate them at their pleasure and yet justify themselves in the eyes of the world'. The German Consul Rössler noted that the 'Islamic gendarmes', who had replaced the former garrison of regular Turkish soldiers, came from nearby Marash and 'were partly personal enemies of the inhabitants of Zeytun'.[21]

The Reverend Dikran Andreasian, the Armenian Protestant pastor at Zeytun, who would later play a central role in the defence of Musa Dagh, told of the mistreatment of the families of men arrested as deserters. Fathers were brutally thrashed. Women and girls were repeatedly raped. Young men who had not deserted were beaten up to ensure that they would not become deserters in future. Property was confiscated. In the end twenty five young men disappeared into the mountains, and took over a monastery as their base. Other deserters joined them. They killed nine gendarmes, and as a result an army of several thousand Turkish troops was dispatched to Zeytun. Instead of resisting, the people of Zeytun agreed both to tell the authorities of the whereabouts of the deserters' stronghold, and to obey the government's instructions. The monastery was attacked and eventually burned to the ground. Many of its defenders managed to escape, while a large number of Turkish soldiers were killed.[22]

The people of Zeytun were deported, as a punishment for their 'revolt'. They experienced a foretaste of the sufferings that many of their fellow Armenians would undergo in the months to come. In a dispatch to the German Foreign Office, the missionary Dr Johannes Lepsius described their fate:

> Of the approx. 27,000 inhabitants of Zeytun in the Taurus Highlands, the male population was deported to the hot Euphrates marshes of Deir es Zor, right in the middle of Arabic Bedouin tribes (500 kilometres to the southeast), while the women, girls and children, on the other hand, were transported to the Angora area (500 kilometres to the northeast); thus, the men were separated from their families by 1,000 kilometres. During transportation the young girls were abducted to Turkish harems and the women were exposed to violation in the Mohammedan villages. While 20,000 Turkish pounds were transferred by the government to make Mohammedan Bosnian settlements in the evacuated area of Zeytun, the Armenians were robbed of their possessions and sent to foreign parts without any means.[23]

A female German missionary recorded that the Zeytun refugees had been sent to 'one of the most unhealthy places in the Vilayet of Konia'. They lacked food and shelter, malaria was rife, and the death rate increased daily. She commented that it was 'cruelly ironic' that the government was pretending to send the Armenians there as colonists when 'they have no ploughs, no seeds to sow, no bread, no abode; in fact, they are sent with empty hands'.[24]

The loss of the legendary mountain stronghold of Zeytun was an immense psychological blow, not only for its uprooted people, but for all Ottoman Armenians. Its failure to resist would later be blamed by many on His Holiness Sahag II, the seventy-five-year-old Catholicos of Sis. Bishop Grigoris Balakian wrote that 'as many times as the Zeytountsis sent messengers to the Catholicos of Cilicia in Adana and the prominent local Armenians in Marash, they always received the same reply: Do nothing extreme that would endanger the lives of the entire Armenian population of Cilicia.' According to the highly respected Egyptian Armenian leader Boghos Nubar Pasha, the Catholicos had been threatened by the local authorities, on the order of the Central Government, 'that if the Zeitounlis refused to capitulate, they would have the whole Armenian population massacred'.[25]

Hovsep Bshtikian, a genocide survivor from Zeytun who was twelve years old at the time of the deportation, remembered how the Catholicos came to the town. He and the other schoolchildren were taken to meet the important visitor: 'He preached, calmed the people down, persuaded them that everything would be alright. He became the reason why the people of Zeytoun did not fight.'[26] The inhabitants of Zeytun obeyed the aged Catholicos out of reverence for him and concern for their fellow Armenians. The prelate and the mountaineers were duped.

In November 1915 Vahram Dadrian visited one of the Zeytun refugees, an 'old mountain lion' named Khacher Aghpar. When asked to talk about his memories of his former home 'he shook his head in refusal and began to curse the Catholicos of Cilicia, who, because he had listened to bad advice, had brought about the surrender of Zeitoun'.

John Halajian's mother attended a *Badarak* (Armenian Liturgy) in Aleppo in 1919, celebrated by Catholicos Sahag for the remnants of his flock. During the sermon the old man confessed the disastrous mistake that he had made, and said: 'I hear the Zeitoonsts are looking for me and want to kill me. Here I am, ready to meet my fate and atone for my sins.'[27]

If the people of Zeytun had been tricked into abandoning self-defence, the inhabitants of Van, after some hesitation and an attempt at compromise, took a different path. The Catch-22 that always trapped the Ottoman Armenians meant, however, that their resistance would be classified by the Young Turk leadership as a 'rebellion' or 'revolt', and thus become the excuse that could be used to justify the full force of genocide.

On 30 March 1915 Djevdet Bey, governor of Van and brother-in-law of Enver Pasha, returned from military operations near the Persian frontier. He immediately began to concentrate his forces around the city. These included 2,000 Turkish soldiers and several thousand irregulars, many of them Kurdish. Shortly afterwards troubles broke out in the village of Shatakh south of Van. The local Dashnak leader and several others were arrested. Some of the Armenians set up barricades in self-defence. Djevdet responded by demanding that all Armenian men between eighteen and forty five be immediately conscripted and sent to work in labour battalions. The Armenians agreed very unwillingly to send five hundred conscripts, though they were deeply concerned about what would happen to them. Vramian, the Armenian parliamentary deputy for Van, argued that the sacrifice of the five hundred was worth making to save the rest of the area's Armenians. He was supported in this by Vardapet Eznik, the leading local ecclesiastic.

On 16 April, at Djevdet Bey's request, Ishkhan, one of the Dashnak leaders, and three bodyguards set out for Shatakh to mediate between the different groups there. That night they were ambushed and killed in the village of Hirj on the governor's orders. The forty six Armenian males in Hirj were also slaughtered, and all the bodies were thrown down a well. Early the following morning, deputy Vramian and Aram, the other Dashnak leader, unaware of the events at Hirj, were summoned by Djevdet Bey. Aram, apparently warned by his colleague, went into hiding. Vramian, confident of his parliamentary immunity, turned up. He was immediately arrested and sent to Constantinople, but was murdered on the way.[28]

Clarence Ussher, the American missionary doctor at Van, became aware of the rumours of massacre and murder that were creating anxiety among the Armenians. He decided to visit the governor (or *vali*) to find out what was really happening, in the hope that he could quiet people's fears:

While I was in his office the colonel of the Vali's Regiment, which he called his Kasab Tabouri or Butcher Regiment, composed of Turkish convicts, entered and said, 'You sent for me.' 'Yes,' replied Jevdet; 'go to Shadakh and wipe out its people.' And turning to me he said savagely, 'I won't leave one, not one so high,' holding his hand below the height of his knee ...

The orders to go to Shadakh may have been a blind; for the regiment turned aside down the Armenian Valley (Haiots Tsore) and destroyed six villages in which there were none but old men, women and children. Many of the criminals had been bandits and outlaws living by their rifles for years and were crack shots. They were mounted, armed with daggers, automatic pistols and modern repeating rifles. Where they saw a mother nursing her babe they shot through the babe and the mother's breast and arm. They would gallop into a crowd of fleeing women and children, draw their daggers, and rip up the unfortunate creatures. I forbear to describe the wounds brought to me to repair.[29]

The Armenian villages and small towns around Van were systematically destroyed and their people savagely slaughtered. Perhaps the cruellest irony was the way in which Turkish propaganda portrayed these atrocities as massacres perpetrated on Turks by Armenians. Ussher noted the way in which Djevdet Bey ensured that the 55,000 Armenians killed in his province were reported as 55,000 'Mohammedans massacred by Christians'. The governor of Van 'described in revolting detail actual atrocities, – women and children, ranging in age from six years to eighty, outraged and mutilated to death, – but made one diabolical change in his description: he said these women were Moslems thus treated by Christians'.[30]

One witness to this cynical inversion of reality was Rafael de Nogales. He stopped overnight in a small town on the way to Van and was told about the threat that the Armenians supposedly presented. On 21 April 1915 he was awakened by gunfire and assumed that the town was being attacked by this apparent enemy. To his surprise he discovered that the shooting actually came from the civil authorities, who were busily slaughtering the local Armenians. When he tried to put a stop to it, he was informed that the provincial governor had issued a decree 'to exterminate all Armenian males of twelve years and over'. That night he sailed across Lake Van, calling in at the holy island of Aghtamar, where 'apart from the corpses of the Bishops and the monks, huddled on the threshold and the atrium of the sanctuary, there seemed to be no human beings on the islet except the detachment of gendarmes which had slain the Christians'.[31]

By Sunday 18 April the Armenians of Van had decided that their only hope of survival lay in resistance to the governor's demands. They formed the Military Committee of Armenian Self-Defence of Van. It included members of all three Armenian political parties. In the days that followed the Armenian Red Cross of Self-Defence opened medical stations that developed into hospitals. The Supply Committee had the responsibility for providing and rationing food. The Women's Committee produced clothing and bandages, and there was a Justice Commission, a Police Corps and even a brass band to boost morale.

Despite this enthusiasm, the Armenians of Van were heavily outnumbered. Djevdet Bey had by now amassed an army of 6,000 infantrymen and between 4,000 and 6,000 Kurdish tribesmen, *chetés* (Special Organization armed ex-convicts) and gendarmes. They also possessed a formidable arsenal, including artillery. The Armenian self-defenders had 1,053 combatants, of whom, Anahide Ter Minassian writes, 'the overwhelming majority ... had no previous military experience, and some had never before held a weapon'. They possessed 506 rifles with 74,824 cartridges, and 549 revolvers, with 39,089 bullets. The Armenian David was facing a Turkish Goliath.

Hostilities broke out on 20 April. Despite acute shortages of ammunition and food (the latter problem exacerbated by the arrival of 5,000 refugees from the countryside), the Armenians managed to hold out until 18 May, when the Russian army and Armenian volunteers entered the city. The euphoria was short lived. On 18 July the Russians decided for strategic reasons to withdraw their forces and evacuate the Armenian population from Van.

More than 100,000 people had to travel more than 200 kilometres to Igdir. Some columns of refugees were attacked. Many children got lost. From Igdir they moved on to the Armenian holy city of Etchmiadzin, where in the next few months 30,000 of them succumbed to illnesses and epidemics.[32]

DECAPITATION: 24 APRIL 1915

In Constantinople, on the evening of 24 April 1915, a plain clothes police officer knocked on Aram Andonian's door. With a polite smile, he invited the Armenian journalist and author to go with him to the local police station, where the Commissar Bey needed a bit of information. It was nothing to worry about, the policeman assured him. It would only take five minutes, and he would soon be home. Similar scenes were taking place at select Armenian addresses all over the capital city. Andonian would later remark that:

> ... our arrests took place with great tact. And this was not surprising. For it was an essential condition for the success of the criminal government's plans to show utmost tactfulness. They had cast their net wide, and they had to exercise extreme caution to ensure a big catch at once. For this reason, it was important not to make noise, to avoid resistance, to avoid incidents, to avoid publicity, to avoid people going underground, and to decrease the number of those who, by various means, might escape from the hell of Turkey.[33]

Some of the fish escaped the net by going into hiding. One was the satirical writer Yervant Odian. In an autobiographical chapter entitled 'The Evil Night', Odian captures the atmosphere among Constantinople's Armenian intellectuals as news of the arrests filtered through to them, first as rumours and then as facts. On the morning of 25 April he began to call on friends, only to find that they had already been taken into custody. He went to the conference room of Holy Trinity Church to find out what was happening. There he heard yet more names of well-known Armenians detained by the police:

> There was now no doubt. If I hadn't been arrested, it was due to a fluke. Maybe the police hadn't found my house. But of course they'd find it today. For safety reasons, I decided not to go to the editorial office.I had already written my articles and could send them there through another person. But where could I hide? 'Don't walk the streets, hide somewhere,' the people I knew at the church advised. I left bewildered. They could arrest me in the street. I walked from Tarla Bashi towards Feridiehn and went to Mr. Bedros Nshanian's house, where I stayed until midday.[34]

Odian was eventually picked up by the police in September. Zabel Yesayan (Essayan), one of the few women on the list, was more fortunate. She managed to escape to Bulgaria and make her way to the Caucasus, where she devoted herself to helping Armenian refugees and orphans. During that time she met the genocide survivor Haig Torosyan, transcribing the testimony that he dictated to her.[35] Among the handful of leading Armenian figures that were not included on the list of those to be detained were the deputies Krikor Zohrab and Vartkes Serengiulian and the Patriarch Zaven Der Yeghiayan. Zohrab and Vartkes would be arrested and brutally murdered later in the year, while Patriarch Zaven would be forced to resign and exiled to Baghdad in 1916.

While Constantinople's Armenian élite were being quietly locked away, Minister of the Interior Talaat, the man responsible for their imprisonment, was having dinner at the American Embassy. When Ambassador Morgenthau questioned him about the Armenians, 'he admitted that they had arrested a great many of them,' adding that he wanted them to leave the city. Talaat told Morgenthau that the intention was to put the Armenians 'among Turks in the interior where they can do no harm'. The following day Lewis Einstein, another American diplomat, recorded in his diary that the Russians had bombarded the Bosphorus forts, and that the Allies were landing at the Dardanelles, while 'there have been wholesale arrests of Armenians – several hundreds are being deported to Angora and Konia'.[36]

Through the imprisonment and deportation of almost all of its most prominent figures, the Armenian community lost its leadership. A similar technique would be used in other cities and towns throughout Turkey to 'decapitate' the Armenians and deprive them of a voice. This would then ease the implementation of a pre-determined policy of extermination. The Swede Alma Johanson, attached to the German Mission at Mush, noted that 'the Vali of Bitlis and the Mutessarif of Moush (the latter being an intimate friend of Enver Pasha) stated officially in last November [1914] that they were only waiting for an opportunity, and that when they would find one, massacres would be started throughout the country and not a soul would be spared'. She also reported that 'in the beginning of April [1915], Ekran Bey, the Adjutant of Major Lange, publicly stated: 'We shall exterminate the Armenian race.'[37] The Armenian self-defence at Van (recast by official Turkish propaganda as a 'rebellion'), combined with the frenetic atmosphere in Constantinople caused by the Gallipoli landings, provided a starting pistol which gave the CUP leaders the opportunity that they had been waiting for. The Genocide of the Ottoman Armenians could begin in earnest.

The celibate priest Father Grigoris Balakian was among those rounded up on the evening of 24 April. He described the atmosphere in the central prison during the night that followed:

> From the deep silence of the night until morning, every few hours Armenians were brought to the prison. And so behind these high walls, the jostling and commotion increased as the crowd of prisoners became denser. It was as if all the prominent Armenian public figures – assemblymen, representatives, revolutionaries, editors, teachers, doctors, pharmacists, dentists, merchants, bankers, and others in the capital city – had made an appointment to meet in these dim prison cells. Some even appeared in their nightclothes and slippers. The more those familiar faces kept appearing, the more the chatter abated and our anxiety grew.[38]

A few of those arrested were the victims of mistaken identity (perhaps because they had the same name as a wanted person). Aram Andonian mentions a harmless impoverished former municipal dog catcher – an illiterate man who suddenly found himself in prison with the foremost Armenian intellectuals in Constantinople.[39]

The 24/25 April prisoners travelled under escort by railway to Ankara, paying for their own tickets. There they were divided into two groups. Those classified as 'political prisoners' were interned at Ayash, four miles west of the city. The 'intellectuals' were sent to Chankiri, sixty miles to the northeast. Their ultimate fate seemed to have been made clear by the Director of State Security, who, while interrogating the psychiatrist Dr Boghosian, had angrily yelled:

If I killed you right here, like a dog, who would come looking for you? If I exterminated the entire Armenian race, as I aspire to do, who would call me to account? I used to think your people were intelligent. You're all stupid, one stupider than the next. Do you think that Europe is going to call me to account? Not at all: Europe's not as hare-brained as you are. Get out of here.[40]

Among those sent to Chankiri was the greatest living Armenian composer and musicologist, the celibate priest Komitas. He had not only made an enormous contribution to Armenian sacred music, but had also collected the folksongs of the rural communities of Ottoman and Russian Armenia. His concerts in major European cities had been hugely successful, and had earned him an international reputation. The American Ambassador Morgenthau thought highly of Komitas, and helped to secure his release. On 17 May the Ambassador noted in his diary:

> Komitas Vartabed called. He and seven other Armenians, out of 200 arrested and sent into interior, had been released. He came to thank me. About 80 of them who were sent to Tchangiri were comparatively free, the rest were sent to Ayash and kept in prison. They had to endure great hardship and had to support themselves. Most are absolutely innocent and the victims of ridiculous mistakes.[41]

Tragically, despite his release, the trauma of arrest and deportation had a lasting impact on Komitas' mind. He showed signs of this on the train journey to Ankara. Father Balakian noticed that Komitas 'thought the trees were bandits on the attack and continually hid his head under the hem of my overcoat, like a fearful partridge'. When they reached Chankiri, Balakian and Komitas sang vespers 'by dim candlelight, behind the high walls of the huge armoury ... with the icy gale blowing through the broken windows'. 'Der voghormya' ('Lord have mercy') is a prayer that always seems to come from the depths of the Armenian soul. Balakian remarks how, when Komitas began to chant the prayer, 'the sobbing was impossible to contain'. His description reflects the depth of the priest-musician's anguish and despair:

> Perhaps Archimandrite Komitas had never in his life sung 'Lord have Mercy' with such emotion. Normally he would sing it ex officio, as solace for the pain, grief and mourning of others; this time he sang out of his own grief and emotional turmoil, asking the eternal God for comfort and solace. God, however, remained silent.[42]

Komitas' mental state was not only disturbed by the impact of his captivity; the loss of his unpublished manuscripts, destroyed after his arrest, was a devastating blow. Knowing of the total destruction the Ottoman Armenian villages where he had quite recently been welcomed by those who sang their folksongs to him, must also have contributed to his illness. In autumn 1916 he was admitted to a mental hospital in Constantinople. After the end of World War I his Armenian friends and admirers moved him to France. He spent the final years of his life, from 1919 to 1935 in mental hospitals there.[43]

For many Armenians, Komitas, the sensitive genius whose mind was destroyed by unhealed trauma, has become inextricably identified with the wounds which the Genocide inflicted on their people: wounds that themselves are not yet healed. Rita Soulahian Kuyumjian, the Canadian

Armenian psychiatrist who has made a detailed study of Komitas' illness, notes how 'survivors of the Armenian Genocide have recognized Komitas's prolonged suffering as a symbol of their own personal and collective anguish, and ranked him among Armenian martyrs'.[44]

While those gathered up on 24 April 1915 languished in Ayash and Chankiri, another group of Armenians were brought before a court-martial in Constantinople. These were connected with the Hunchak party, and included the veteran leader Paramaz, who had previously been imprisoned by the Russians on many occasions, Aram Achekbashian, who had helped to arrange the 'Kum Kapu' demonstration in 1895, and Dr Benneh Torosian, who combined a medical practice with political activism. Speaking on behalf of the defendants, Paramaz said of the Ottoman Armenians: 'Among the groups making up Turkey, we were the most dedicated and productive, and we were the ones you forced to suffer most.' Twenty of the accused, including Paramaz, Aram Achekbashian and Dr Benneh Torosian, were found guilty of 'high treason and separation' and condemned to death. Their hanging, at half past three in the morning on 15 June 1915, took place secretly in the courtyard of the War Ministry. The result of the trial was used by Young Turk propagandists to fuel anti-Armenian conspiracy theories.[45]

Among the Armenian prisoners at Ayash was Agnouni, a Dashnak politician who had worked closely with Talaat in the past, hiding him in his house and thus saving his life during a political crisis. Shortly before the arrests, when Agnouni was ill in bed at home, Talaat had called on him to see how he was. Now, even though Agnouni bombarded the Interior Minister with personal telegrams, Talaat did not deign to reply to them. The Dashnak politician was among a group of six Ayash prisoners who were tortured and killed by *chetés* of the Special Organization on the road to Diarbekir. Once he had realized that there was no hope of reprieve, Agnouni told his companions, 'I am not sorry for my death since one day death will find us all, but I am sorry that we were deceived by these Turkish criminals.' Apart from the Hunchak leader Murad, who was executed separately at Kayseri, the other Ayash prisoners were slaughtered in August 1915, along with twelve hundred Armenians from Ankara.[46]

The prisoners at Chankiri were also gradually sent away to be murdered. Aram Andonian was fortunate enough to fall from a carriage and break his leg, thus ending up in hospital, which saved his life. On Friday 20 August five of the prisoners were transferred to Ankara. They included two of the finest Western Armenian poets, Daniel Varoujan and Rupen Sevag. The Chankiri CUP arranged to have them ambushed by a gang of Kurds. Its leader was a man named Halo. His daughter's life had been saved by Rupen Sevag, who was a doctor, only a month before. The attack took place on the Saturday, with the co-operation of the police who were supposed to be guarding the prisoners. Balakian describes the atrocity:

> ... the Kurds took our five friends to the edge of a brook that runs through the nearby valley and tripped them, so as not to damage their clothing. Then they drew their daggers and attacked them, ripping their bodies apart and slashing their legs and arms and other sensitive parts. Only Varoujan defended himself, and as a punishment, after gutting him, the criminals dug out the eyes of the patriotic poet.[47]

Varoujan and Sevag were not the only poets to perish as a result of the arrests of 24 April 1915. Among those murdered at Ayash was Siamanto, who had so graphically depicted the horror of the Adana massacres.

The two leading Armenian politicians who had not been arrested during the Constantinople raids did not remain free for long. On 26 April Krikor Zohrab had been part of a delegation that tried in vain to persuade both the Grand Vizier and Talaat to treat the Armenians with less severity. The reaction of the Young Turk leaders made it clear that both Zohrab and Vartkes were in danger, but neither of them was willing to contemplate leaving the country. When an influential person offered Zohrab the possibility of escape, he responded: 'To whom do you want me to abandon this people, without leadership or a chief? I do not want to leave; it is my duty to remain on the front lines to the very last.' On 1 June, as news of the appalling massacres in the eastern provinces came in, Zohrab said that he would use his position as a deputy in parliament to publicly call Talaat to account for his actions. The following evening the Armenian played cards with the Interior Minister, and then went home. Two hours later he was arrested.[48]

Vartkes was taken into custody on the same night. A Special Correspondent of the *Times* later recalled an incident from September 1913 during which 'Talaat ... explained to me jokingly that there was nothing that he would not do for his friend Vartkes'. The journalist observed that 'the relationship between the two men seemed, indeed, to be those of two chums, and my impression was afterwards confirmed by the language of Vartkes himself'.[49] By June 1915 Talaat's 'chumminess' (always a somewhat dubious quality) had disappeared, at least as far as Vartkes was concerned. He and Zohrab were sent to be tried by the court-martial at Diarbekir. They were murdered near Urfa during the journey.

On 6 August Henry Morgenthau, the American

Ambassador, heard an account of the two men's deaths from a visitor who had just returned from Urfa. He named the murderer as 'Ahmed Bey', and said that Zohrab's body had been shot four times with a pistol.[50] Rafael de Nogales had once dined with this killer:

> A gentleman called Achmed Bey was seated upon my right, dressed in well-cut English tweeds. He spoke several languages perfectly, was a member of some of the best clubs in Constantinople, and had spent many years in London. With his aristocratic manners and his rather blasé expression, anyone might have taken him for one of the snobs driving four-in-hand along the avenues of Hyde Park. Yet this Achmed Bey was none other than the notorious bandit Tcherkess-Achmed, leader of a troop of Circassian guerrillas who later on killed the Armenian deputies Zorab, Vartkes and Daghavarian in the Devil's Gulch, by the Governor's order; and one year afterwards was hanged in Damascus by Djemal Pasha, who feared that later on his own complicity in that assassination might be revealed![51]

Balakian wrote that 'having received news of the killings, Zohrab's supposed friend Talaat sent word to Zohrab's wife that her husband, who had a heart condition, had suffered a stroke on the way to Diyarbekir'.[52]

---

[1] Kaligian, *Armenian Organization*, p.236; Walker, *Armenia*, pp.198-9; Zaven Der Yeghiayan, *My Patriarchal Memoirs* (Barrington, Rhode Island: Mayreni Publishing, 2002), p.58; Gust, *The Armenian Genocide*, p.200.

[2] Vahakn N. Dadrian, *The History of the Armenian Genocide: Ethnic Conflict from the Balkans to Anatolia to the Caucasus*, sixth, revised edition (New York: Berghahn Books, 2007), pp.220-1.

[3] Verjiné Svazlian, *The Armenian Genocide: Testimonies of the Eyewitness Survivors* (Yerevan: Gitoutyun Publishing House of the National Academy of Sciences of the Republic of Armenia), p.112.

[4] Akçam, *A Shameful Act*, pp.130-6; Dadrian and Akçam, *Judgment* at Istanbul, p.299; Kévorkian, *The Armenian Genocide*, p.184.

[5] James L. Barton (compiler), *'Turkish Atrocities': Statements of American Missionaries on the Destruction of Christian Communities in Ottoman Turkey, 1915-1917* (Ann Arbor, Michigan: Gomidas Institute, 1998), p.177.

[6] Vahram Dadrian, *To the Desert: Pages from My Diary* (Princeton, New Jersey: Gomidas Institute, 2003), pp.10-11.

[7] Maria Jacobsen, *Diaries of a Danish Missionary: Harpoot, 1907-1919* (Princeton, New Jersey: Gomidas Institute Books, 2001), p.41.

[8] W.E.D. Allen and Paul Muratoff, *Caucasian Battlefields: A History of the Wars on the Turco-Caucasian Border 1828-1921* (Nashville, Tennessee: The Battery Press, 1999), pp.284-5. Üngör gives the Turkish losses as 78,000 out of 90,000 (*The Making of Modern Turkey*, p.59).

[9] Zaven, Patriarchal Memoirs, p.63.

[10] Akçam, *A Shameful Act*, pp.143-4.

[11] Atkinson, *Harpoot Diaries*, p.80.

[12] Svazlian, *The Armenian Genocide: Testimonies*, p.552.

[13] Clarence D. Ussher, *An American Physician in Turkey: A Narrative of Adventures in Peace and in War* (London: Sterndale Classics, 2002), p.117.

[14] Hayg Toroyan a Zabel Essayan, *L'Agonie d'un people* (Paris: Classiques Garnier, 2013), pp.27-8.

[15] Ara Sarafian (compiler), *United States Official Records on the Armenian Genocide 1915-1917* (Princeton, New Jersey: Gomidas Institute, 2004), p.502.

[16] Nogales, *Four Years Beneath the Crescent*, pp.127-8.

[17] Kévorkian, *The Armenian Genocide*, pp.310,312.

[18] Sarafian, *United States Official Records*, p.255.

[19] Gust, *The Armenian Genocide*, pp.663-5.

[20] Gust, *The Armenian Genocide*, pp.147, 156-7; Toroyan and Essayan, *L'Agonie d'un people*, p.29.

[21] James Bryce and Arnold Toynbee, *The Treatment of Armenians in the Ottoman Empire, 1915-1916: Documents Presented to Viscount Grey of Fallodon by Viscount Bryce*, Uncensored Edition, edited by Ara Sarafian, second edition (Princeton, New Jersey: Gomidas Institute, 2005),p.492; Gust, *The Armenian Genocide*, p.161.

[22] Bryce and Toynbee, *The Treatment of Armenians*, pp.490-1.

[23] Gust, *The Armenian Genocide*, p.213.

[24] Bryce and Toynbee, *The Treatment of Armenians*, pp.498-9.

[25] Grigoris Balakian, *Armenian Golgotha* (New York: Alfred A. Knopf, 2009), p.45; Bryce and Toynbee, *The Treatment of Armenians*, p.479.

[26] Svazlian, *The Armenian Genocide: Testimonies*, p.433.

[27] Dadrian, *To the Desert*, p.115; John Halajian, *A Written Bridge: Love Letters for Armenia* (Mustang, Oklahoma: Tate Publishing and Enterprises, 2013), p.147.

[28] Anahide Ter Minassian, 'Van 1915' in Richard G. Hovannisian (editor), *Armenian Van/Vaspurakan* (Costa Mesa, California: Mazda Publishers, 2000), pp.216-8.

[29] Ussher, *An American Physician in Turkey*, pp.127,129.

[30] Ussher, *An American Physician in Turkey*, p.177.

[31] Nogales, *Four Years Beneath the Crescent*, pp.58-60.

[32] Ter Minassian, 'Van 1915', pp.225-43.

[33] Aram Andonian, *Exile Trauma and Death: On the road to Chankiri with Komitas Vartabed*, edited by Rita Soulahian Kuyumjian (London: Gomidas Institute and Tekeyan Cultural Association, 2010), pp.4-5.

[34] Yervant Odian, *Accursed Years: My Exile and Return from Der Zor, 1914-1919* (London: Gomidas Institute, 2009), p.16.

[35] Agop J. Hacikyan (co-ordinating editor), *The Heritage of Armenian Literature, Volume III: From the Eighteenth Century to Modern Times* (Detroit: Wayne State University Press, 2005), p.793; Toroyan and Essayan, *L'Agonie d'un people*, p.7.

[36] Morgenthau, *United States Diplomacy: Diaries*, pp.215-6; Lewis Einstein, *Inside Constantinople: A Diplomat's Diary During the Dardanelles Expedition, April-September, 1915*, revised edition (London: Gomidas Institute, 2014), p.7.

[37] Sarafian, *United States Official Records*, p.363.

[38] Balakian, *Armenian Golgotha*, p.57.

[39] Andonian, *Exile Trauma and Death*, p.6.

[40] Kévorkian, *The Armenian Genocide*, p.254.

[41] Morgenthau, *United States Diplomacy: Diaries*, p.231.

[42] Balakian, *Armenian Golgotha*, pp.66,73.

[43] Gurgen Gasparian (editor), *Komitas Vardapet (1869-1935)* (Yerevan: Sargis Khachents Printinfo, 2009), pp.240-1.

[44] Rita Soulahian Kuyumjian, *Archeology of Madness: Komitas, Portrait of an Armenian Icon* (Princeton, New Jersey: Gomidas Institute, 2001), pp.2-3.

[45] Rita Soulahian Kuyumjian, *Teotig: Biography* and Teotig, *Monument to April 11* (London: Gomidas Institute and Tekeyan Cultural Association, 2010), pp.136-7; Kévorkian, *The Armenian Genocide*, pp.254-7.

[46] Balakian, *Armenian Golgotha*, pp.90-5; Andonian, *Exile Trauma and Death*, pp.40-1.

[47] Balakian, *Armenian Golgotha*, p.101.

[48] Kévorkian, *The Armenian Genocide*, pp.252-3,533-4.

[49] 'Wholesale Murder in Armenia: Exterminating a Race', *The Times*, Thursday, September 30, 1915 in *The Times of the Armenian Genocide: Reports in the British Press: Volume I: 1914-1919*, edited by Katia Minas Peltekian (Beirut: Four

Roads, 2013), p.84.

[50] Morgenthau, *United States Diplomacy: Diaries*, pp.296-7.

[51] Nogales, *Four Years Beneath the Crescent*, p.70.

[52] Balakian, *Armenian Golgotha*, p.105.

4. THE DESCENT INTO HELL

PORTRAYING GENOCIDE

From 24 April 1915 the true horror of genocide spread across Ottoman Turkey, starting with the Armenian heartland in the east, and then spreading out to other communities. Genocide dehumanizes its victims. It turns unique individuals – mothers, fathers, brothers, sisters, grandfathers, grandmothers, aunts, uncles, cousins, daughters, colleagues, friends and loved ones – into numbers. A thousand dead in this village, twenty thousand in that town, four hundred here, forty thousand there – as the corpses pile up, the people whom those corpses once were become statistics. Only a handful of traumatized survivors remember them as they once were. Some of the photographs in the *UCLA Historic Armenian Cities and Provinces* volume about Tsopk/Kharpert provide a graphic illustration of this process of dehumanization.

The pictures taken before the Genocide show ordinary extraordinary individuals sharing in everyday life: the

Armenian Band of Mezre French College, for example, or a patriarchal extended family from the village of Hoghe. The Armenian professors, teachers and students of Euphrates College and of the Central Schools of Kharpert and Mezre, male and female, sit or stand demurely for their class photos, as people do in educational establishments all over the world. Then there are the seriously bearded leaders of the Christian denominations in Kharpert, joining the American Consul and the Catholicos of Sis, for a souvenir picture of the latter's visit to his home area. There are also photographs of Armenian craftsmen and women: a rug weaver, textile workers, silk thread drawers, shoemakers, carpenters and metal smiths.[1]

The strict orders of both the Turkish and the German authorities meant that no photographs of the annihilation of the Armenians were supposed to exist. Some courageous people, perhaps most notably the German officer Armin T. Wegner, disobeyed this decree and managed to take and smuggle out pictures of the Armenians' suffering.[2] The Genocide photographs in the UCLA volume provide an appalling contrast with those portraying the society that previously existed. Ragged, filthy Armenian conscripts in a labour battalion stare with dead eyes at the camera, holding the long-handled shovels with which they will soon almost certainly be asked to dig their own graves. A convoy of Armenians on foot, with nothing except the clothes they are wearing, are escorted from the town by armed men. A half-naked youth with legs like sticks tries to hide his (or her?) face from the camera; a starved corpse, also half-naked, lies in the street – behind it a tiny child sits amid piles of rags and hopeless, helpless figures huddle against a wall. A mother, in tattered garments, clasps the hand of her similarly clad son, as they look numbly down at the body of his younger brother. An orphan boy shields his eyes as he stares at the camera, while a starving child with emaciated legs and arms, protruding ribs, a swollen belly, and a head that seems too big gives a piercing look that penetrates the soul. These are people from among what once had been, as Paramaz declared at his trial, 'the most dedicated and productive' of the different ethnic groups making up Ottoman Turkey.[3]

The reality of the experiences undergone by Armenians caught up in the Genocide was so appalling that they were, and still are, extremely difficult to convey to those who have never gone through such experiences. This is illustrated by the trials and tribulations of the real-life heroine of a silent film made to draw attention to the Armenian tragedy. Arshaluys Mardiganian was a sixteen year old Armenian girl from Chemishgezak, north of Kharpert. She arrived in America on 5 November 1917, looking for her brother. Her parents and other brothers and sisters had been slaughtered during the Genocide. Arshaluys herself had suffered at the hands of Turks, Chechens and Kurds, before eventually reaching safety in Erzerum after its fall to Russian forces.

An Armenian couple from New York helped her in her search for her surviving sibling by putting advertisements in newspapers. These led to interviews by journalists, which attracted the attention of a screenwriter named Harvey Gates. He and his wife became the young Armenian's legal guardians. They transformed her name from Arshaluys into Aurora. With the New York Armenians acting as interpreters, she told her story to Gates. He wrote it up for publication, and it appeared as *Ravished Armenia: The Story of Aurora Mardiganian – the Christian Girl who lived through the Great Massacre*. Aurora, who had originally been hoping to find work in a New York dressmaking factory, was instead whisked off to Los Angeles by Mr and Mrs Gates. Taking advantage of her minimal English, they asked her to sign a paper. It turned out to be a contract by which she agreed to take part in a film of the book. She would be paid $15 a week – hardly film-star wages. One of the advantages of a silent movie was that the heroine's very limited grasp of English was not a problem.

Anthony Slide makes an important point about both the book and the film, which also applies to some other accounts by survivors or witnesses of the Genocide:

> Atrocity after atrocity – ethnic cleansing in its most brutal and savage form – is recorded in the narrative, so much so that the reader is forced to question if all these crimes could have been committed against one girl, one family. The reader is tempted, as were contemporary critics of the book and subsequent film, to wonder if Aurora Mardiganian was perhaps not a real person but rather an amalgam of all the tortured, suffering and murdered young women of Armenia. In reality, both the book and the film are relatively sanitized versions of what Aurora Mardiganian actually suffered and witnessed.

The most dramatic and shocking image in the film showed a row of naked Armenian girls crucified on wooden crosses. It proved too powerful and shocking for the British censors and too politically sensitive for the Foreign Office, and had to be cut when the film was shown in London in 1920. However, when Slide interviewed Aurora Mardiganian in 1988, she revealed that the reality had been even more horrifying:

> 'The Turks didn't make their crosses like that. The Turks made little pointed crosses. They took the clothes off the girls. They made them bend down. And after raping them, they made them sit on the pointed wood, through the vagina. That's the way they killed – the Turks.

Americans have made it a more civilized way. They can't show such terrible things.'

She also confided another memory which was too traumatic to be included in the book and the film:

'My uncle's wife had her two-and-a-half-year old son with her. The Turks, they took a knife and cut open her abdomen. They said, this is how we are going to end all you people. They pulled out a fetus from her. Put it on a stone. They took the end of the gun which they had, which was heavy, and started to pound and pound and pound her baby.'

Yet even the film, which was screened under two titles, *Ravished Armenia* and *Auction of Souls*, was derided by one up-and-coming young critic, who declared himself 'bored' by it, as well as being 'heartily sick of the screen's exploitation of atrocities under any guise'. As for the girl who had been a genuine victim of atrocities, he dismissed her with the brutal comment: 'Miss Mardiganian isn't camera interesting'.[4]

One problem for those depicting genocide, which the film critic's snide remarks underline, is that it is possible to become surfeited with real-life horror, as well as with semi-fictional or 'factional' reconstructions of it. The term 'compassion fatigue' comes to mind. Yet there are times when realities, however unpleasant, have to be faced up to and described, if only for the sake of those who are victims of them. One of those who attempted to do this was the eighteen-year-old Eastern Armenian poet Eghishe Charents. In 1915 he was serving in a volunteer Armenian unit with the Russian army. As he and his comrades penetrated into Ottoman Armenia they came across scenes of devastation caused by the genocide. These are reflected in his long poem 'Dantesque Legend', first published in Tiflis in 1916.[5]

On one occasion, described in the poem, Charents and his fellow soldiers entered the smouldering ruins of a village on the shores of Lake Van. He and a friend found a vineyard. They were about to pick some grapes to quench their thirst when they came across the body of an old man. He had been strangled. His blood stained the fruit, while his eyes stared at them. Charents' friend collapsed, asking him for water. The poet found the vineyard well, and let down the bucket. He drew it up again:

Another minute and suddenly
as if spirits rose to dance about me

I looked, stiff-eyed, into the clear
water of the pail in which also
half disintegrated parts of a body
rocked calmly.
Barely controlling the scream in
my throat I left the well,

Like a drunken waverer
pursued by ghosts. Both of us ran then
seeing neither vineyard nor sea
where the devil, with his poisons, slept.

From there Charents and his companions entered the 'Dead City'. They went into a house: the 'wide holes' of its windows gaped 'like, sunless dugout eyes'. Inside they found the naked, bloodstained body of a woman who had been raped and murdered. The young soldier-poet was traumatized by the sight. Spending the night 'in one of the houses of the Dead City,' he hallucinated 'in the candleless dark':

> Before me the dead bayed
> groaning, moaning around their fires.
>
> Their dead bodies with blue legs,
> yellow breasts, swollen and blood-
> spattered buttocks,
> danced, staggering before
> my terror-filled eyes
> in the grave-pit dark.[6]

The horror of the reality of the Genocide, and its impact on individual human beings, brought Charents to the verge of mental breakdown.

If Charents' waking dream emphasizes the degradation and the dehumanization of the Genocide victims, there is one artist who has succeeded in producing a series of paintings which express the horror of what happened, while preserving the humanity and individuality of those who died and those who survived. A series of pictures by the French Armenian painter Jansem are on display in the Museum of the Armenian Genocide in Yerevan. They show the victims as they were, in all their vulnerability and agony. They are not easy paintings to look at. On my visits to the Museum, I have found that I can only keep my eyes on them for a few seconds at a time.

Why? Most of the figures are naked, stripped of everything, as the deportees were. Many are dead. Some have very clearly been treated brutally: starved, beaten or raped, like the woman in the 'Dead City', whose tragic corpse brought Charents to the edge of insanity. Not wishing to be prurient may be a factor in my turning away –

but there is also something much deeper: a desperate desire to cover their nakedness, and take away their sense of desolation, shame and despair. Above all, there is a longing to show these anguished figures the respect that is the right of every human being – a respect which they were so savagely denied. A hundred years have passed. I cannot reach out to them. Yet a passionate desire remains to ensure that they are not forgotten.[7]

ARRESTS AND AFTER

In Constantinople the authorities had rounded up the Armenian élite on 24 April. In the eastern provinces they used the same technique of arresting the leaders of local Armenian society. The usual pretext was suspected subversion, though it was also a convenient way of extracting money from the victims. Some of the allegations made would have been comic, if their results had not been so tragic. In Diarbekir an unfortunate old man was dragged into custody for having 'dangerous' books in the house. They included an atlas and a physics text book. The former, according to the corporal who arrested him, was 'a more terrifying weapon than all the guns and cannons of the army,' because it 'gives the locations of all the cities, villages, rivers, and roads in Turkey'. The latter 'tells you all you need to know about how to make gun-powder, bullets, and dynamite'.[8]

In prison the Armenian captives were subjected to a variety of brutal tortures. One of the most common was the bastinado. After talking to two of the victims, Frieda Wolf Hunecke, a German missionary in Everek, sent a detailed description to Ambassador Wangenheim:

The prisoner is placed in stocks (as used during Roman times) with 2 gendarmes on each side and 2 at the foot end who now take turns in beating the soles of his feet with sticks as long as their strength lasts. During Roman times, 40 blows was the highest, but here 200, 300, 500 or even 800 blows were supposedly administered. The foot begins to swell enormously, then bursts open on top due to the repeated blows, and thus the blood is spurted away. The prisoner is then dragged back to the jail and put to bed by the remaining prisoners ... As they have meanwhile become unconscious, probably due to the continued blows, cold water is poured over their heads to revive them ... The next day, or more correctly the night because these maltreatments always take place both in Kayseri during the night as well as in Everek, the treatment was repeated despite the swelling and despite the wounds.[9]

Witnesses reported that in Everek prisoners were beaten to death in the courtyard every evening, while the local governor, sipping a glass of cognac, looked on appreciatively. The chest of one of the victims, Asadur Minasian, was covered with live coals. His killers then made coffee on it.[10]

The principal Armenians in Kharpert were arrested on 1 May 1915. A survivor described their ordeal to the American missionary Isabelle Harley. Among their many torments, their hair, beards and moustaches were pulled out, and their finger and toe nails extracted. They were hung by the arms for a day and a night, and beaten into insensibility. One of the Euphrates College professors, unable to stand the agony, managed to smuggle out a desperate message to Dr Atkinson at the American Hospital: 'Send us poison, we cannot endure it any longer.'

'The poison was not sent,' Miss Harley comments tersely.[11]

In Diarbekir, the province of Dr Reshid Bey, a governor notorious for his ruthlessness and cruelty, the tortures which the leading local Armenians suffered in prison were horrific:

> Hagop Bozo [the blacksmith] and some of his associates were shoed and compelled to run like horses. They drove red-hot horseshoes in the breast of Mihran Bastajian and his associates. They forced some others to put their heads under big presses, and then by turning the handles they crushed the heads to pieces. Others they mutilated or pulled their nails out with pincers. In other more slow cases, they first pulled out the nails with pincers, then pressed the fingers under a heavy press after which they cut the fingers one by one. Darakji Hagop was operated on his private parts. Others were flayed alive. Some were taken to the slaughter house, killed and their flesh distributed as if for sale to the butchers! Police Ohan and his friends were crucified and had long nails driven through their hands and feet ...[12]

The clergy were not spared. When one priest was arrested, his wife was gang-raped by ten gendarmes and almost died. Several priests in Diarbekir were stripped, covered in tar, and dragged through the streets. According to a German officer, when horseshoes were nailed to the feet of the Bishop of Sivas, the governor commented cynically: 'He's a bishop! So you can't let him go barefoot!'[13]

The most horrific end was reserved for primate Chlghadian, the senior Armenian cleric in Diarbekir. After his teeth had been pulled out, his cheeks were pierced with red-hot irons, and his eyes gouged out. He was then dragged through the streets of the city as an object of public entertainment and amusement. The procession was accompanied by musicians playing their instruments. It ended in the courtyard of the principal mosque. There, in the presence of a large crowd and the civil and military authorities, the primate was sprinkled with petroleum and set on fire. Before the flames could kill him, they were extinguished. Horribly burned, but still alive and suffering appalling pain, he was dumped in the stables of the Government Hospital. It was there that an American missionary, Dr Smith, 'found him in a totally unrecognisable condition, writhing in the midst of terrible pains with a black piece of dirty rag thrown over him, and past all hopes of life'. The governor claimed that primate Chlghadian had died of typhus fever. Henry Riggs, another American missionary, described the martyred primate as 'a man of unusual courage and aggressiveness, who, at the beginning of these troubled times, had taken active steps to appeal to Constantinople for pity on his people, and who, even in prison, had continued to make efforts in their behalf'.[14]

Over six hundred prominent Armenian prisoners from Diarbekir were selected to be sent down the river Tigris to Mosul on 30 May 1915. Their families watched as the men, chained or roped together, were escorted through the streets of the city, singing songs of farewell. At the river bank they were put onto rafts, and set off downstream, guarded by militia and Circassians led by Major Shakir Bey. The Major suggested that the prisoners hand over any gold that they possessed to him, as they were about to travel through an area renowned for Kurdish brigands. The Armenians duly entrusted £6000 in gold to the Turkish officer. They were unaware that Governor Reshid Bey had made an arrangement with Amero, a local Kurdish chief, to slaughter them on the way. This was duly done. On 10 June the German Consul reported that empty rafts had been sighted on the river. Soon afterwards the remains of the murdered men began to float past Mosul.[15]

One of the worst atrocities in Diarbekir took place later in the year. On 22 October the Danish missionary in Kharpert, Maria Jacobsen, noted in her diary: 'All the Armenian children who had been collected in Turkish children's homes have been taken away in ox-carts and thrown in the river.'[16] She is presumably referring to an incident which Mugerditchian describes in grim detail. Four hundred Armenian orphans, between one and three years old, had been being looked after in the former Protestant school in Diarbekir, which had been converted into an orphanage for them. Then, one morning, two hundred of these infants were taken to a bridge south of the city and hurled into the fast-flowing river Tigris. The remaining two hundred suffered an even more appalling fate, after being taken to a village named Karabash:

Some of the babies were seized by their legs and pulled in opposite direction[s] so forcibly that they were torn in two. On others the sharpness of the swords or bayonets of their butchers was tried, and real competitions were started as to who could cut at one stroke an arm or a leg or a head or even the baby's body. Others were thrown in the air and caught on lances, while others were thrown to some exceptionally wild shepherd-dogs to be torn to pieces. The official representatives of the Turkish government who assisted at this heinous scene were most delighted and followed the whole procedure with perfect satisfaction.[17]

Mugerditchian does, however, note one Turkish functionary who was revolted by this mass infanticide. The province's Inspector of Health, Dr Ismail Bey, is recorded as having told his friends that God may forgive all sins, all the massacres, all the atrocities which Turks committed against the Armenians, but he will never, never, never forgive them for what they did to those innocent, blameless little babies. Such plain speaking was unwise in Reshid Bey's Diarbekir. The Inspector was swiftly removed from his post, and he and his family were escorted to Constantinople to face the wrath of the central authorities.[18]

A large number of prominent local Armenians were hanged in Kayseri (Kesaria). On Monday 14 June the American mission's steward came across the bodies of eleven of them, left on the gallows in the market place as a warning to their fellow Armenians. Teotig records the names of fifty-three of the victims, some of whom were members of political parties, while others seem to have had no political involvement at all. The best-known was not a Kayseri man: the parliamentary deputy Hampartzum Boyajian (Murad) was leader of the Armenian Hunchak party, and had been previously held with the other Constantinople political prisoners at Ayash. On 15 August Patriarch Zaven wrote that more than eighty people had now been hanged in the town, and that 'the hanged persons' families – their mothers, fathers, and wives – have the duty to take the corpses down from the gallows'.[19]

In Bitlis men and boys over ten years old were rounded up and imprisoned on 23 June. An American missionary remembered that 'in most cases the men went quietly, trusting that they would soon be released'. She added that 'the government succeeded perfectly in deceiving the people with its assurances'.[20] Two days later Djevdet Bey and the eight thousand men of his *kesab taburi* (butcher battalions) reached Bitlis. He extorted £5,000 in gold from the wealthiest Armenians, and then had them hanged. The rest of the men were taken out in groups to a remote place in the mountains and slaughtered, having been forced to dig the trenches into which their bodies were then thrown. The only ones to survive were a handful of artisans whose skills were essential for the war effort. Even the smaller male children did not escape; 'all the boys between one and ten were taken from their families, thrown into a huge pit, doused with paraffin and burned alive in the governor's presence[21] Rafael de Nogales estimated that 'about fifteen thousand Armenians perished in the city of Bitlis and its environs in one day'.[22]

The arrests of Armenian community leaders and their torture, combined with the killing of large numbers of men, were a foretaste of what would follow. They left the Armenians in the eastern provinces increasingly demoralized and helpless. In Marsovan the provincial governor told a Muslim audience shortly before the deportations began: 'You have no hesitation about killing a chicken: can you have any hesitation about killing these people, – the enemies of your country? They do not deserve the consideration that a chicken does.' Shortly afterwards the 1,200 Armenian men held prisoner in the city's barracks were taken out by night in batches, killed with axes (to save ammunition) and buried in trenches that had been prepared in advance.[23]

As the horrors of impending deportation became more and more apparent, a potential means of escape was dangled in front of the Armenians. It was suggested that they might save themselves by giving up their Christian faith and converting to Islam. Christianity is at the heart of Armenian identity: Armenians are very conscious of belonging to the first Christian nation. It created an acute inner crisis for some – others were less troubled. It was reported that in Marsovan the governor and the commandant of gendarmes had received thousands of Turkish pounds in bribes from wealthy Armenians who wished to save themselves from deportation by becoming Muslims.[24]

However, for many what had seemed like a lifeline frequently turned out to be an illusion. Thus Dr George White, the President of Anatolia College, reported that in Marsovan 'in all about 1,200 persons, mostly women and girls ... accepted Moslem registry'.[25] The sad fate of some of them was described by another American, Miss Frances Gage:

> Only four weeks before I left [Marsovan], a company of young brides with their little boys, all of whom had become Mohammedans, were sent away. The order had come privately, not to the Governor but to the police, that women who had boys, no matter if they were babies in arms, should be deported with their children. Of that category there were perhaps three or four hundred in the city, and about 60 wagon-loads were chosen out at this time to go ... This whole batch was killed in the mountains, on the other side of the plain from the city. Their birth certificates were found, and the burial had been so badly done that the bodies of little children were left on the ground, and the arms and legs of the corpses in the ditches protruded.[26]

Sometimes there were doubts about the sincerity of converts. On 22 July 1915 Bertha Morley heard a story from Amasia. Four hundred Armenian families there had converted to Islam. The suspicious authorities rang the bell of the Armenian church. All but fifteen of the convert families flocked to the building. As a result they were deported. In Birejik, between Aintab and Urfa, the entire Armenian population, apart from the parish priest, became Muslims. Their main motivation seems to have been fear about their future. They even demolished the church belfry as proof of their enthusiasm for their new religion. The desperate uprising of Armenians in Urfa kindled doubts among the authorities, and the converts of Birejik were deported on 25 November 1915.[27]

Those converts who did manage to survive often lived hidden, fearful lives. In August 1918 the Danish missionary Maria Jacobsen visited one of the three such families in Osmania:

> We found the old man with his wife and children. It was hard to see the fear in which they are living. When we spoke in Armenian, they literally shook with fear in case anyone might have heard us. Every time they heard a sound in the street they thought the Turks were coming for them ... Their hearts were bitter. They said it was the Christians, the Germans, who had killed them. They said that God had left them, so they had denied the Saviour and become Turks. They knew no joy nor peace.[28]

'LET THEM WAIT AND SEE WHAT DEPORTATION IS.'

Henry Riggs, the American missionary from Kharpert, protested about the treatment of Armenians to the local parliamentary deputy, Hadji Mehmet Effendi. The Young Turk politician replied: 'The Armenians know what massacre is, and think they can bear that. But let them wait and see what deportation is. They never dreamed of being deported. They will soon learn how much worse it is than massacre!' American Consul Leslie Davis, while not sharing the deputy's hatred of Armenians, wrote to Ambassador Morgenthau expressing a similar view of the nature of deportation in 'the peculiar conditions of this isolated region':

A massacre, however horrible the word may sound, would be humane in comparison with it. In a massacre many escape but a wholesale deportation of this kind in this country means a lingering and perhaps even more dreadful death for nearly every one. I do not believe it possible for one in a hundred to survive, perhaps not one in a thousand.[29]

An anonymous American teacher from Marsovan reported that the Armenians themselves regarded deportation as 'worse than a massacre', adding that 'no one knew what was coming, but all felt that it was the end'.[30]

Another American, Isabelle Harley, visited an encampment of three thousand people, 'mostly women and children', who had been brought on a winding route through the mountains from Erzerum, and were temporarily halted at Mezereh:

Tired, sick, hungry, beaten, dirty, vermin invested, frightened, hunted, broken-hearted creatures they were pushed on the next day and then on, and on, and on, and on, not knowing where they were going nor when the end would come. It was the plan of the government to keep this up until the last had dropped. This was what they called deportation![31]

The group of deportees whom Isabelle Harley met had already been travelling for forty-five days. There had originally been eighty thousand of them. However, the men and older boys had been taken away and killed. Many young women and girls had been abducted. Others had died from dehydration or starvation.

Separating out the men and older boys from the women and children and then slaughtering them was an essential part of the organization of deportation from the eastern provinces. Colonel Stange reported to the German Military Mission in Constantinople that, out of the first convoy of deportees that had left Erzerum on 16 June 1915, 'all the men, with very few exceptions have been murdered', while 'nothing certain is known about the grown-up girls'. The fate of the men was described in a letter from a young woman who was herself abducted by a Turk. The convoy (which included some of the wealthiest Erzerum Armenians) had crammed themselves into a stable for three days, having paid $880 to the Kurdish village chieftain for the privilege. Their guards persuaded them to move on, but they had hardly gone a mile when they came under attack from Kurds, Turks and gendarmes: 'All the men were killed outright except one who was wounded and made his way to Harpoot where he became a Moslem to save what was left of his life.'[32]

A survivor from a convoy of five hundred families which left Erzerum two days later wrote that two hundred of the men were killed at Kamakh and two thousand more at Malatia. Those at Malatia were told by their executioners (Kurds and Turkish gendarmes): 'You will now die, but this is not our fault; the government demands it.' They were then stripped, beheaded with knives or axes, and their bodies disposed of in a chasm. A hundred and fifteen other men were more fortunate. They knew enough Kurdish to bribe their captors with promises of money, and were allowed to escape and rejoin the women and children. One of them was Dr Sarkis Manukian, who wrote down his experiences for the German Consul in Aleppo.[33]

Sometimes the killing was indiscriminate. The Armenians of Erzindjan, like their fellow deportees elsewhere, had to sell their prized possessions for derisory amounts. Their convoys began to leave during the first week in June. Two German Red-Cross nurses heard from some Turkish soldiers how these exiles had been slaughtered at Kamakh gorge:

> ... the defenceless Armenians had been massacred to the last one. The butchery had taken four hours. The women threw themselves on their knees, they had thrown their children into the Euphrates, and so on. 'It was horrible,' said a nice-looking young soldier. 'I could not fire, I only pretended.' For that matter we have often heard Turks express their disapproval and their pity. The soldiers told us that there were ox-carts all ready to carry the corpses to the river and remove every trace of the massacre.

Six days later the same two German nurses, out for an evening stroll with a male companion, met a gendarme who had been escorting a large convoy of deportees from Baibourt:

> He narrated to us with appalling vividness, how one by one the men had been massacred and cast into the depths of the gorge: 'Kezzé, kezzé, geliotlar! (Kill, kill, push them over).' He told how, at each village, the women had been violated; how he himself had desired to take a girl, but had been told already that she was no longer a maid; how children had had their brains battered out when they cried or hindered the march. 'There were the naked bodies of three girls; I buried them to do a good deed,' was his concluding remark.[34]

Mrs Victoria Khatchadour Barutjibashian was among the four or five hundred members of the third convoy to leave Baibourt. She was a well-to-do widow, and was accompanied by her mother and her eight-year-old daughter. For the journey they took with them some money, four diamond rings, and three horses laden with provisions. After they had been travelling for a couple of hours, the convoy was ambushed by a large number of brigands and villagers. Mrs Barutjibashian's horses, food and money were stolen. The men were taken aside, one by one, and every male over fifteen years old was killed over the next few days. All the attractive women were abducted, including the widow's sister. She had a baby which was thrown away by her captor, only to be snatched up by a Turk who disappeared with it. Mrs Barutjibashian's mother, worn out by the journey, had to be abandoned by the roadside.

Some wagons containing Turkish war widows on their way to Constantinople came up to the convoy of deportees. They agreed to take the Armenian widow and her daughter with them, on condition that they both became Muslims. They accepted. The journey took them along the banks of the Euphrates and across the plain of Erzindjan. Mrs Barutjibashian mentions that they were horrified to see the mutilated bodies of women, girls and small children, and that their escort 'were doing all sorts of awful deeds to the women and girls that were with us, whose cries went up to heaven'. All the remaining children under fifteen were thrown in the Euphrates. The gendarmes and irregulars shot and killed the ones who could swim. No Armenian was left alive in Erzindjan, apart from women and girls who had accepted Islam. They passed fields and hillsides dotted with rotting corpses. Six women in Muslim dress, carrying babies, whom they met on the road turned out to be Armenian men in disguise. They were executed on the spot. The widow and her daughter eventually reached Constantinople, where Mrs Barutjibashian gave her testimony to Ambassador Morgenthau.[35]

On Monday 5 July eight hundred Armenian men were

arrested in Kharpert, Mamuret-ul-Aziz and the surrounding villages. They included the pharmacist for the Kharpert missionaries. On the Tuesday the prisoners were tied together in groups of fourteen, and marched off to a Kurdish village under strict guard. Some of them spent the night in the mosque. The following day they were taken to a valley a few miles away and made to sit down. The gendarmes shot some of them, and finished off the rest with bayonets and knives. The young pharmacist was at the end of the line, and managed to break away. He escaped through a ravine and across the fields and eventually reached the sanctuary of the American hospital. He was later smuggled to safety in Russia.[36]

On the Black Sea coast there were deportations by sea as well as by land. In the Ottoman Parliament Chamber of Deputies on 11 December 1918, Hafiz Mehmet, a lawyer who was deputy for Trebizond, described how he had witnessed Armenian women and children being squeezed into a barge at Orlu and taken out to be drowned at sea. He added that the governor of Trebizond had carried out similar drownings. The former Italian Consul-General in Trebizond, writing in a Rome newspaper in August 1915, referred to 'children ... placed by hundreds on board ship in nothing but their shirts, and then capsized and drowned in the Black Sea and the River Deyirmen Deré'. The American Consul in Trebizond mentioned Armenian men being taken out to sea in caiques which returned empty a few hours later.[37] At least one of those involved later suffered a personal disaster, which he interpreted as a divine judgment on his part in the atrocities:

A boatman, fleeing with his family from Trebizond, met with a storm, lost his property and his family and barely escaped himself to Samsoon in a half crazy condition, where he ran through the streets crying, 'See the way the Lord takes revenge? Last year I drowned scores of Armenians in the sea in Trebizond.'[38]

Colonel Stange reported that of the Armenians deported by land from Trebizond, 'the men were led aside into the mountains and massacred with the help of military troops, while the women were driven on in a deplorable state to Erzindjan'. Carl Schlimme, another German soldier, came across some of them on 26 June 1915:

> ... a large group of expellees passed through Erzindjan, consisting of only women and children. Many among them were ill and well advanced in pregnancy; many women and most of the children were half naked. They carried bundles of grass and ate this because they had nothing else. Some begged me for money to buy bread. When I gave them some they were beaten by the gendarmes. This group headed towards the Kamakh gorge.[39]

Bergfeld, the German Consul at Trebizond, was virulently anti-Armenian. He wrote that 'anyone who knows the Orient will agree with me that the Armenians are blessed with hardly a trait that humans find attractive'. Nevertheless, even he admitted that 'the excesses that took place during their deportation – the mass murders of the men, numerous rapes of women and children, and theft of their possessions – cannot be condemned severely enough'.[40]

---

[1] Richard G. Hovannisian (editor), *Armenian Tsopk/Kharpert* (Costa Mesa, California: Mazda Publishers, 2002), pp.15,23,224-6,254-5,300,302-4.

[2] Peter Balakian, *The Burning Tigris: The Armenian Genocide* (London: William Heinemann, 2004), pp.258-9.

[3] Hovannisian, *Armenian Tsopk/Kharpert*, pp.341-5;Kévorkian, *The Armenian Genocide*, p.256.

[4] Tigran, *Prior to the 'Auction of Souls'*, edited by Sossi Ghazarian-Kevonian (Yerevan: the editor, 2008), p.76.Anthony Slide, *Ravished Armenia and the Story of Aurora Mardiganian* (Lanham, Maryland: The Scarecrow Press, 1997), pp.5-7,11-12,14-15.

[5] Yégiché Tcharents, *Légende Dantesque (1915-1916), bilingual Armenian-French edition*, translated by Serge Venturini and Élisabeth Mouradian (Paris: L'Harmattan, 2010), pp.7-8.

[6] Eghishe Charents, *Land of Fire: Selected Poems*, edited and translated by Diana Der Hovanessian and Marzbed Margossian (Ann Arbor, Michigan: Ardis Publishers, 1986), pp.70-2.

[7] The paintings have been published as a catalogue: *Jansem*, with a preface by Raymond Blanc (Yerevan: Museum of the Armenian Genocide, 2002).

[8] Dadrian, *To the Desert*, pp.64-5.

[9] Gust, *The Armenian Genocide*, p.252.

[10] Kévorkian, *The Armenian Gemocide*, pp.514-5.

[11] Barton, *'Turkish Atrocities'*, pp.65-6.

[12] Thomas K. Mugerditchian, *The Diyarbekir Massacres and Kurdish Atrocities* (London: Gomidas Institute, 2013), p.35.

[13] Gust, *The Armenian Genocide*, p.320; Annick Asso, *Le cantique des larmes: Arménie 1915: Paroles de rescapés du genocide* (Paris: La Table Ronde, 2005), p.153.

[14] Henry H. Riggs, *Days of Tragedy in Armenia: Personal Experiences in Harpoot, 1915-1917* (Ann Arbor, Michigan: Gomidas Institute, 1997), pp.53-4; Mugerditchian, *The Diyarbekir Massacres*, pp.35-6; Kévorkian, *The Armenian Genocide*, pp.361-2.

[15] Gust, *The Armenian Genocide*, p.252.

[16] Jacobsen, *Diaries*, p.99.

[17] Mugerditchian, *The Diyarbekir Massacres*, pp.49-50.

[18] Mugerditchian, *The Diyarbekir Massacres*, p.50.

[19] Barton, *'Turkish Atrocities'*, p.122; Teotig, *Monument to April 11*, pp.112-13, 158-9; Simon Payaslian, 'The Fateful Years: Kesaria during the Genocide' in Richard G. Hovannisian (editor), *Armenian Kesaria/Kayseri and Cappodocia* (Costa Mesa, California: Mazda Publishers, 2013), p.299; Zaven, *My Patriarchal Memoirs*, pp.94-5.

[20] Grace H. Knapp, *The Tragedy of Bitlis, being mainly the narratives of Grisell M. McLaren and Myrtle O. Shane* (London: Sterndale Classics, 2002), pp.38-9.

[21] Kévorkian, *The Armenian Genocide*, p.341.

[22] Nogales, *Four Years Beneath the Crescent*, p.115.

[23] Sarafian, *United States Official Records*, p.526; Barton, *'Turkish Atrocities'*, pp.78-9.

[24] Sarafian, *United States Official Records*, p.526.

[25] Barton, '*Turkish Atrocities*', p.81.

[26] Bryce and Toynbee, *The Treatment of Armenians*, p.373.

[27] Morley, Marsovan 1915, pp.36-7; Toroyan and Essayan, *L'Agonie d'un people*, pp.103-4.

[28] Jacobsen, *Diaries*, pp.218-19.

[29] Riggs, *Days of Tragedy in Armenia*, p.140; Sarafian, United States Official Records, p.456.

[30] Sarafian, *United States Official Records*, p.143.

[31] Barton, '*Turkish Atrocities*', p.68.

[32] Gust, *Armenian Genocide*, pp.328-9; Barton, '*Turkish Atrocities*', p.23.

[33] Gust, *Armenian Genocide*, pp.489-50.

[34] Gust, *The Armenian Genocide*, pp.623-4.

[35] Sarafian, *United States Official Records*, pp.157-8.

[36] Sarafian, *United States Official Records*, pp.632-3.

[37] Dadrian and Akçam, *Judgment at Istanbul*, p.40; Bryce and Toynbee, *The Treatment of Armenians*, p.317; Sarafian, *United States Official Records*, pp.179-80.

[38] Sarafian, *United States Official Records*, pp.526-7.

[39] Sarafian, *United States Official Records*, pp.526-7.

[40] Gust, *The Armenian Genocide*, pp.329,736.

5. 'ARMENIA WITHOUT ARMENIANS'

WOMEN AND CHILDREN

In September 1915 a Turkish guide took Leslie A. Davis, the American Consul in Kharpert, to inspect the area around Lake Goeljuk, an idyllic place where missionaries and their families had often spent enjoyable holidays before war broke out. What he discovered horrified him. The deep valleys around the lake had been used to slaughter huge numbers of Armenian deportees. He returned a few weeks later with Dr Atkinson from the American Hospital, to make a more thorough investigation. He reported that:

> We estimated that in the course of our ride around the lake, and actually within the space of twenty-four hours, we had seen the remains of not less than ten thousand Armenians who had been killed around Lake Goeljuk. This, of course, is approximate ... I am sure, however, that there were more, rather than less, than that number; and

it is probable that the remains that we saw were only a small portion of the total number in that vicinity ... That which took place around beautiful Lake Goeljuk in the summer of 1915 is almost inconceivable. Thousands upon thousands of Armenians, mostly innocent and helpless women and children, were butchered on its shores and barbarously mutilated.[1]

The massacres at Lake Goeljuk and elsewhere greatly lessened the number of Armenians from the eastern provinces who reached their officially proclaimed destination in the deserts of Syria and Mesopotamia. Older boys and young and middle-aged men had either been conscripted for labour gangs (which usually meant a slightly deferred death sentence) or separated from the women and slaughtered. A handful of old men remained with the convoys, but they mostly succumbed to heat, thirst, hunger or exhaustion. Those from the Armenian plateau who reached Aleppo were almost all women and children, unlike those from the western provinces, where the men were allowed to travel with their families (though the situation of many of the latter would change once they were moved to the concentration camps in the desert).[2]

Toroyan gives a graphic description of the arrival outside Aleppo of the first convoy of deportees from the Armenian heartland:

They were only women and children, about two thousand in number. There wasn't one man among them. Terribly emaciated, skin burned brown, clothed in rags, hungry, thirsty, they seemed like madwomen. The dust of the soil was stuck to their faces in such a way that, from a distance, one had the impression of an earthy mass, all stuck one to the other, as if they could never be separated. They were standing there petrified, they didn't know where to go. From time to time a woman sighed, moving her head, or a child fell to the ground, exhausted, and they waited.[3]

These women and children had witnessed the most appalling atrocities. Vahram Dadrian tells of the experiences of his cousin Eugenie from Samsun, one of only thirty survivors from a convoy of deportees that had once numbered thousands. After two days, all the males over thirteen in her caravan of well-to-do Armenians were taken on one side and killed. The women and children were stripped of their belongings. The horse-drawn carriages where taken away, and they had to continue on foot. The soldiers thought that the women might have some hidden jewellery, and conducted more than twenty 'inspections' of them. Eugenie said that 'during the process of these inspections they committed unspeakable acts of violence on them'. All the attractive girls and widows were abducted by Turkish or Kurdish peasants. Many of the Armenian women committed suicide, others died as a result of the hardships of the journey. The sick, the elderly, children and those who lagged behind were killed. One day all the boys between nine and thirteen were slaughtered. Eventually the handful of survivors reached Aleppo.[4]

Mary Riggs was able to give an even more detailed account of the fate of the Armenians deported from Kharpert on 1 June 1915. The convoy consisted of three thousand people, 'mostly women, girls and children'. They were escorted by seventy policemen and a certain Faik Bey. The following day, this 'Turk of influence' collected 400 Turkish pounds from the deportees, promising to keep it safely for them. He said that he would protect the Armenians by going with them as far as Urfa – but instead immediately decamped with the money. By the third day Arabs and Kurds had begun to abduct women and girls. The policemen of the escort repeatedly raped women openly and encouraged the local tribesmen to commit robbery, rape, murder and kidnapping. On the fourth day three of the principal men were killed. Five days later the horses (paid for to Malatia) were sent back to Kharpert, and ox-carts had to be hired. One of the policemen absconded, kidnapping an Armenian woman and her two daughters.

On day thirteen the convoy reached Malatia, only spending an hour there. The policemen took 200 Turkish pounds from the deportees, and then abandoned them, leaving them in hands of a Kurdish chieftain. On the fifteenth day, while they were in the mountains, the Kurds slaughtered 150 of the men. Another caravan of refugees from Sivas, Egin and Tokat joined them, swelling the numbers to eighteen thousand. The Kurds continued to pillage the deportees. The abduction of girls and women persisted relentlessly. On the fortieth day they reached a tributary of the Euphrates and saw the bodies of more than 200 men in the river. To prevent their suffering the same fate, each man in the convoy had to pay the local village chief a Turkish pound.

Twelve days later the Kurds from another village stripped them of everything, including their clothes. The naked deportees were scorched and burned by the sun as they stumbled on. They were given no bread or water for the next five days, and many died of thirst. When they eventually reached a fountain the policemen stopped them drinking from it, forcing the deportees to buy a cupful of water for between one and three Turkish pounds – and not always giving them the water after taking their money for it. Elsewhere some women jumped into a well, trying to get at the water, and were drowned. Their fellow deportees still drank from the corpse-filled well. Some Arabs showed compassion and gave many of them rags to cover their nakedness. Mary Riggs notes the ways in which the naked women preserved the little money they had left: 'some kept it in their hair, some in their mouths and some in their wombs'. This led to brutal searches by their attackers.

By the sixtieth day there were only three hundred left from the eighteen thousand. Four days later the remaining men were burned alive, along with the sick women and children. When they finally reached Aleppo ten days later, only thirty five women and children were left out of the three thousand deportees that had set out from Kharpert, and only a hundred and fifty from the entire convoy of eighteen thousand. The deportation had proved a cruelly drawn-out exercise in the extermination of men, women and children. C.S. Graber summed up its purpose in the title of his book about the Genocide, *Caravans to Oblivion*.[5]

Accounts of the convoys often refer to the appalling agony of women who gave birth during the deportation, and of the fate of their newborn offspring. One description was given by a compassionate German official of the Baghdad Railway:

> Women who bear children along the way suffer the worst fate. They are hardly given enough time to give birth to their child. One woman had twins during the night. The next morning she had to continue on foot, carrying two children on her back. After marching for two hours she collapsed. She had to put the children down under a bush and was forced by the soldiers to continue marching with her other travelling companions. Another woman gave birth during the march, had to move on immediately and collapsed, dead ... A newborn child was found when cleaning up a khan that had been abandoned by a

transport just an hour earlier. In Marash, three newborn children were found bedded in manure in the Tash khan.[6]

This grim recitation could be paralleled a great many times from the statements of other witnesses.

The sexual abuse of Armenian women and girls was one of the most marked and atrocious features of the Genocide. In some cases they were forced into brothels, set up for the pleasure of Turkish officers or officials of the Committee of Union and Progress. In Trebizond, Nael Bey, the loathsome CUP representative, helped himself from among the Armenian children: 'He himself chose ten of the best looking girls and kept them in a house for his own pleasure and amusement of his friends'. In Bitlis three hundred Armenian women were held under guard in the Armenian cathedral. There they were forced to pleasure officers and soldiers on their way to the front. As a result the women contracted venereal disease. They thus became a liability to the military, and were killed, mostly with poison. Women were also trafficked. Kévorkian describes the first example of a public sale of young Armenian women. It took place at Mardin on 15 August 1915, and 'buyers had to pay from one to three Turkish pounds per head, depending on the beauty and age of the female on offer.' George White in Marsovan also mentions prices demanded 'for eligible young women', adding 'I know, for I heard the conversation of coarse men engaged in the traffic'.[7]

Rape is constantly referred to in descriptions of the deportation convoys. Consul Rössler from Aleppo sent the Imperial Chancellor in Berlin a report from a reliable Armenian source, who stated that:

It must also be noted that apart from the young girls and

women who were kidnapped, 25 per cent of those whose appearance was more or less pleasing were taken to one side by force during the day or night by the gendarmes accompanying them, by Kurds and Turks, and raped: some of those who were more beautiful even by 10-15 men. In this way, a whole crowd of women and girls were left along the way.[8]

The trauma caused for those who survived was appalling. Rössler mentions a woman who tried to commit suicide on the railway line after being raped by eight Chechens. She was rescued by a German engineer, who brought her to safety in Aleppo. A German schoolmaster in the same city describes a fourteen-year-old girl, also rescued by a railway official: 'The child had been raped so often in one night by Turkish soldiers that she had completely lost her mind.'[9]

The women who were abducted from the convoys often went through a long series of ordeals. Mrs Anna Papazian was part of the second convoy to leave Erzerum. It was attacked by the thugs of the Special Organization. Her husband, a photographer and Sunday School teacher, was stripped and stoned to death. Their youngest child was smashed against a rock. Mrs Papazian fainted, but was then 'rescued' by an officer on horseback. He took her to a village and raped her. She passed out again, and was unconscious for three days. Coming round, she managed to get permission to look for her two remaining children, a boy of four and a girl of six who had both been with her mother-in-law. The old lady had been taken away, and presumably killed. Mrs Papazian was, however, able to recover her children. For the next eight months she was passed from Turkish officer to Turkish officer (twelve in all), but succeeded in keeping the children with her. Finally she managed to escape, and was sheltered by some friendly

Kurds, until she and her family were rescued by Armenian volunteers with the advancing Russian army.[10]

The Danish missionary Maria Jacobsen noted in her diary the story of Digin Vershin, 'a very beautiful young Armenian woman, who had lived in England for 12 years'. She and her husband had come back to Ottoman Armenia on a visit, and had been trapped there by the outbreak of war. Although they had official papers authorizing their safe travel, the convoy of which they were a part was attacked by Kurds, who killed all the men. Digin Vershin was abducted by a particularly brutal Kurdish chieftain. 'A few weeks ago', Jacobsen wrote, 'the Kurd began to talk about sending her away, saying he regretted that he had not killed her.' He was persuaded to allow her to come to stay with the Danish missionaries. Eventually, because of a falling out within his family, the Kurd allowed her to go free. Later Digin Vershin attempted to escape behind the Russian lines, but was caught and imprisoned by the Turks.[11]

Mothers were sometimes persuaded to hand over their daughters, rather than allowing them to undergo the suffering of the convoys. Before the deportation from Vank, some of the wives of important local dignitaries went there to pick out three Armenian girls. Bertha Morley recorded in her diary that:

Yesterday they went again ... they stayed some time enjoying the shade etc., then picked out four girls – three small and one large. Sirouhi Pestimaljian and her sister being two of them. They talked with their mothers of the horrors of the way and how they would certainly be stolen by Kourds or Circassians or rough villagers, and how much better it would be if they would give them to her. So, as our caller reported, mothers were persuaded to consent to let their daughters be brought back to

Turkish houses. None of the mothers slept but cried all night and pinched their flesh.[12]

Heranush Gadaryan was a young Armenian girl who was part of a convoy of women and children. She was forcibly separated from her mother, and taken by a Turkish corporal to be a servant. She was given the name Seher and brought up as a Muslim. Her brother Khoren had been taken off to be a shepherd, and was renamed Ahmet. Another survivor was her aunt Siranush who had married a Kurd – perhaps the one who stole her away from the convoy. Heranush/Seher was married off to the nephew of the corporal's widow. Then a letter arrived. Her mother had survived the convoy. Her husband had been working in America when war broke out, and she had now been reunited with him. Heranush's father came to Aleppo to look for his son and daughter. Khoren joined him there, and went to America, but Heranush/Seher's husband would not allow her to go with him. She settled down to be a Turkish Muslim housewife. It was only towards the end of her life that she told her granddaughter, the human rights lawyer Fethiye Çetin, about her Armenian origins. Later, Fethiye discovered that 'people in the town had referred to my grandmother and others like her as 'the leftovers of the sword'. They'd be talking about someone, and they'd say, 'That one was a leftover of the sword, too.'[13]

RESISTANCE

While there were many Turks who saw the CUP policy of eliminating the Armenians as an opportunity for settling old scores, self-enrichment or sexual exploitation, there were others who reacted differently. In Kharpert, Riggs noted that 'the more intelligent Turks for the most part remained either indifferent or positively friendly towards the Armenians'. The penalties for sheltering Armenians were, however, severe. On 10 July 1915 the Commander of the Turkish Third Army sent a telegram to the provincial governors of Sivas, Trebizond, Van, Mamuret-ul-Aziz, Diarbekir and Bitlis ordering that 'heads of households who shelter or protect Armenians are to be executed in front of their houses and it is imperative that their houses be burned down'. A fortnight later, Maria Jacobsen wrote in her diary that 'the crier has shouted today from the mosques and around the streets that any Turk who hides an Armenian will be hanged and his house burned'. All the houses in Kharpert, from the governor's residence to the poorest hovel, were to be searched.[14]

Despite this edict, not all in the community were cowed. Maria Jacobsen tells of an aged sheikh who fell on his face at the governor's feet, and pleaded for the Armenians: 'It is enough now. Let the innocent go free. Our Koran does not allow such cruelty.' The governor told the old man that the persecution would stop – but continued it nevertheless. Even more courageous was the Kharpert Turk who had an Armenian hidden in his house, and refused to hand him over. His response to the authorities was: 'I have known him since he was a boy and I love him like a son. I know he is innocent, and I will not hand him over. If you want him, then you must first take and kill me.' The Danish missionary commented that 'it is good to meet such people, who really suffer with the Armenians, but unfortunately there are very few'.[15]

In August 1915 Max von Scheubner-Richter, a German consular official in Erzerum, reported a conversation with 'a very respected and influential Bey', who remarked that 'although Armenian massacres had taken place formerly, they were generally restricted to battles amongst the men, but that now, against the instructions in the Koran, thousands of innocent women and children are being murdered'. Two months later, two teachers at the German Secondary School in Aleppo described the appalling conditions in which Armenian deportees were suffering and dying in a building across a narrow alleyway from the school. They noted that 'there are indeed numerous, decent Muslims who condemn this mass murder of innocent women and children as a sin against the commandments of God the Merciful'.[16]

Reports of actions taken against the Armenians caused such profound religious qualms among a group of leading Muslims in Kastamonu province that they confronted their governor, telling him: 'We have heard that they are driving the Armenians, along with their women and children, from the surrounding provinces into the high mountains and slaughtering them [there] like sheep in a slaughterhouse. We do not want such a thing [to occur] in our country. We fear Divine punishment.'[17]

A few courageous Turkish officials opposed the annihilation policy espoused by Talaat, Enver and their henchmen. Consul Rössler informed the Imperial Chancellor:

In the Vilayet of Diyarbekir, a Kaymakam was given verbal orders on the procedure against the Armenians. He refused to carry them out if they were not repeated in writing, whereupon he was dismissed and murdered on the way to Diyarbekir ... Not one, but rather several public officials were supposedly killed because they did not act mercilessly against all Armenians in their district.[18]

Those who were murdered for opposing the Genocide included Hüseyin Nesimi Bey (mayor of Lîce), Ali Sabit El-Suweydi (vice-mayor of Beşiri), the mayor of Derik, Nuri Bey (mayor of Midyat), and the *kaymakam* (area governor) of Bafra. Other officials were dismissed or transferred elsewhere. Only the *mutesarif* of Kütahya, Faik Ali Bey, succeeded in preventing the deportation of the Armenians of his district, apparently because he had the strong support of the local Turkish population and of two of the important families of the area.[19]

Apart from the self-defence at Van, there were other instances of Armenians resisting the policy of extermination. These often tended to reflect a sense of profound desperation among those who took part in them. Mush provides one such example. For six days from 9 July 1915 the irregulars of the Special Organization systematically wiped out the Armenian villages of the plain of Mush with characteristic brutality. Each village was surrounded. Groups of men were rounded up, tied together and butchered in an orchard or a field. The killers would pick out the most desirable young women or children, and shut the rest up in a barn and burn them to death. Yeghiazar Karapetian from Sasun described how the Sunday of Vardavar (the Feast of the Transfiguration) was turned into the 'Sunday of Mardavar' ('the burning of people') for many of those who lived on the plain: 'about ten to twelve thousand Armenian women, children, old and young people were burned down to ashes in the stables and barns of Krdagom, Khasgyough and Hunan.'[20]

Another survivor, Shoger Abraham Tonoyan, from Vardenis village in the plain of Mush, was fourteen years old when her community was destroyed. She would never forget the horror of what she witnessed:

On the day of Vardavar, 1915, the Turkish askyars brought Chechen brigands from Daghestan to massacre us. They came to our village and robbed everything. They took away our sheep, oxen and properties. Those who were good-looking were taken away ... together with all the males in the town ... They shut people in the stables of Malkhas Mardo, they piled up stacks of hay round them, poured kerosene and set them on fire. Sixty members of our great family were burned in those stables ... Only my brother and I were saved ... From the beginning they took away the pretty young brides to Turkify them and also they pulled away the male infants from their mothers' arms to make them policemen in future. The stable was filled with smoke and fire, people started to cough and to choke ... People ran, on fire, to and fro, struck against the walls, trod upon the infants and children who had fallen on the ground ... During that turmoil the greatest part of the people choked and perished. The roof of the stable collapsed and fell upon the dead.

After the collapse of the stable roof, Shoger managed to escape with her little brother. They slipped past the soldiers, who were too absorbed in a victory dance to notice them.[21]

In Mush itself, on 11 July, the town crier went round to announce a government order that all males over fifteen were to leave for Urfa, and should therefore register in preparation for this. Alma Johansson, a Swedish missionary in the town, reported that almost all of the few Armenian men left thought that they would be killed if they allowed themselves to be deported: 'they decided that they would rather die together in their houses, and only if the soldiers attempted to enter with force would they sell their lives as dearly as possible'. The following morning the bombardment of the town began. After three days the cannons fell silent, but the shooting lasted for a whole week.

Turkish gendarmes and officers boasted to the Swedish missionary about the fate of their opponents. The few men caught alive were taken outside the town and shot. The women and children were either locked in houses in nearby villages and burned to death or drowned in the river. Alma Johansson's conclusion was that 'except for a small number of women whom the Kurds or Turks took for themselves, almost everything in the entire Mush region which could call itself Armenian has been exterminated ...' However, the stolen Armenian women seem to have clung on to their faith in secret. Robert Hewsen describes an experience in a former Armenian village that is now a suburb of present-day Mush: 'an obliging Muslim opens the door of a storage room where he shows a niche marked with crosses and blackened with candle smoke. Here, he relates, the old women used to come and pray when he was a boy'.[22]

Apart from Van, the one successful example of Armenian self-defence was in the coastal area around Musa Dagh (Mount Moses). Two factors made a difference in this instance. One was the presence of the Reverend Dikran Andreasian, who came from Yoghanolouk, at the foot of Musa Dagh. He had been the Armenian Protestant pastor in Zeytoun when its people were deported. Because he was not a native of that area, he had been allowed to return to his home town. His experience meant that he had no illusions about the implications of deportation. What also differentiated Musa Dagh from most other Armenian communities was its proximity to the sea. That would eventually prove to be the salvation of its brave band of fighters.

Some of the Armenians of the area agreed to trust the government's promises, and were escorted by Turkish guards to Antioch and beyond. The others retreated to the heights of Musa Dagh, taking their sheep and goats, and any weapons that they could find. They were attacked by two hundred Turkish soldiers whom they managed to drive back. The Turks brought up a field gun, but a young Armenian sniper managed to pick off four of the gunners manning it. As extra support for the besiegers, who now numbered three thousand regular soldiers, the inhabitants of nearby Moslem villages were recruited and armed. They seemed to be in a position to overwhelm the defenders. However the Armenians used the cover of night to creep round the enemy position, and attacked the Turkish camp in the rear. The result was complete confusion in the Turkish ranks. They retreated, leaving behind rifles, ammunition and a mule.

By now the horde besieging the mountain had swollen to some fifteen thousand. Not only were the Armenians massively outnumbered, they were also running short of food. The only solution would be to escape by sea. The women made two enormous flags to attract the attention of passing ships. One was a white flag inscribed in English with black letters 'CHRISTIANS IN DISTRESS: RESCUE'. The other had a large red cross against a white background. On the fifty-third day of the siege a warship appeared off the coast.

Movses Panossian, one of the defenders of Musa Dagh, described what happened next:

The Kerekians' son was a good swimmer; he dived into the sea and swam to the ship.

There was a small metal box hung from his neck, containing a letter written in French. From the ship, they had been watching with field glasses; they had seen him. They helped him to get on board the ship. Movses had knelt, crossed his face to make them understand he was a Christian, for he could not speak French. He had given the captain the written letter; they read it, understood that about five thousand Armenian Christians of Moussa Dagh were waiting for God's salvation.

The battleship was the *Guichen*. It was soon joined by three other French cruisers. The defenders of Musa Dagh were safely evacuated and taken to Port Said in Egypt.[23]

In 1933 the Austrian Jewish writer Franz Werfel wrote his epic novel *The Forty Days of Musa Dagh*, based on the events on the mountain in 1915. It was inspired by seeing 'maimed and famished-looking' Armenian refugee children in Damascus. By the time that the book appeared Hitler's shadow had begun to darken Europe. Werfel's theme of the attempted annihilation of the Armenians now seems like a prophetic glimpse of the Holocaust to come. Peter Sourian observed that 'when at the very end, Werfel has Gabriel [Bagradian, the hero of the book] thinking that 'to be an Armenian is an impossibility,' one is tempted to think that it could easily be Werfel himself, the European Jew writing under siege, really, in 1933, and thinking desperately how impossible it is to be a Jew'. The film rights of the novel were acquired by Metro-Goldwyn Mayer. Edward Minasian has chronicled the extraordinary saga of the Turkish government's pressure on the United States State Department over several decades, which prevented the film being made.[24]

Unlike the defence of Musa Dagh, the siege of Shabin-Karahisar had a tragic outcome. In this community in the province of Sivas there were 1,200 Armenian families. The ancient fortress of Shabin-Karahisar was easily accessible from the Armenian quarter. On 15 June 1915 several hundred of the wealthiest Armenian citizens were arrested.

This led to the start of armed resistance on the following day. Over five thousand Armenians, three quarters of whom were women and children, took refuge in the fortress, which was swiftly surrounded by Turkish forces. On 3 July the defenders repulsed an attack by between 5,000 and 6,000 Turkish soldiers. A week later the supply of food in the fort was almost exhausted. An attempted break out by some of the Armenian fighters led to their being wiped out. On the morning of 12 July the Armenians surrendered. The men were shot, and the women, children and the very old were deported.[25]

The resistance at Urfa (the ancient Edessa) was particularly tragic. The city had suffered two massacres in 1895. In the first, in October, several hundred people died. The second, two months later, had been one of the most appalling of the Hamidian atrocities: three thousand Armenian Christians took shelter in their cathedral, which, under Islamic law, should have been respected as a place of sanctuary. They were burned to death.[26] Such an event could not be forgotten after only twenty years. In addition, since the beginning of the deportations, convoys of Armenians had been routed through the city. The Reverend F.H. Leslie, an American missionary in Urfa, reported to Consul Jackson at Aleppo on 6 August 1915:

> For six weeks we have witnessed the most terrible cruelties inflicted upon the thousands of Christian exiles who have been daily passing through our city. All tell the same stories and bear the same scars ... The poor weak women and children died by thousands along the road and in the khan where they were confined here. There must be not less than five hundred abducted now in the homes of the Moslems of this city and as many more have been sexually abused and turned out on the streets

again. They have even abused these girls openly on the streets and before the eyes of the foreigners.

Leslie was aware of the impact of this on the local Christian community, writing that they 'seeing and knowing very well what has happened to these other exiles are not in a mood to accept exile themselves, and if it is attempted they may resist'.[27]

Two Turkish policemen searching for arms were killed on 19 August, and this sparked a massacre of several hundred Armenians. The Armenians barricaded themselves into their quarter of the city. The use of church bells had been banned in Urfa since the massacre of December 1895. On 29 September 1915 they rang out again, as a symbolic signal of the start of the uprising. Among the soldiers sent to suppress it was a Bavarian captain, Eberhard Count Wolffskeel von Reichenberg, who was serving as General Fakhri Pasha's chief of staff. Wolffskeel was impressed by his opponents. He wrote to his wife that 'the entire defence is very well prepared and led'.[28] Mgrdich Yotneghperian, in charge of the Armenian defenders, was hit in the knee by shrapnel on 15 October. He refused to surrender, and was carried on a stretcher from position to position, encouraging his fighters. The Armenian quarter was subjected to relentless shelling by Wolffskeel's field artillery, and by 19 October most of it was in Turkish hands. Resistance ended on the evening of 23 October. Yotneghperian killed himself before he could be taken captive. The surviving male defenders were hanged.[29]

The women and children were deported, apart from those who were abducted before the start of the journey. Elvesta Leslie was told by a reliable informant that 'less than a hundred' of the deportees reached Rakka on the Euphrates, and that 'the girls who arrived there were in a terrible condition'. As they were walking, they were told that they could return home, and so the convoy would turn round and set off back towards Urfa. Then, a couple of days later, they would be forced to retrace their steps towards Rakka again. 'In this way,' Leslie remarks, 'they were obliged to travel over the same road five or six times'. They became more and more exhausted, and their numbers grew smaller as they were literally walked to death.[30]

TOWARDS THE 'FINAL SOLUTION'

As the deportations spread from the Armenian plateau to other provinces, railway trucks were increasingly used to transport deportees, though those who were unable to pay a sufficient amount were still organised into walking convoys. Mrs Anna Birge, an American, gave an eye-witness account of some of these trains on the Anatolian Railway:

> At every station where we stopped, we came side by side with one of these trains. It was made up of cattle-trucks, and the faces of little children were looking out from behind the tiny barred windows of each truck. The side-doors were wide open, and one could plainly see old men and old women, young mothers with young babies, men, women and children, all huddled together like so many sheep or pigs – human beings treated worse than cattle are treated.

Mrs Birge had the opportunity to speak to some Armenians from a train which had been stranded at a station for three days. Their Turkish guards had prevented them from buying food. She was told how 'twenty babies had been thrown into a river as a train crossed – thrown by the mothers themselves, who could not bear to hear their little ones crying for food when there was no food to give them'. Another woman, after giving birth to twins in a crowded cattle truck, had thrown herself and her newborn babies into the water.[31]

A German witness paints a similar picture of misery. On 12 August 1915, W. Spieker, a Baghdad Railway engineer, went to the Damascus Station in Aleppo to watch a thousand women and children being loaded into cattle wagons. He commented that 'in Germany, livestock is given more space than these poorest of the poor'. He added that '90% of these people had death written on their faces'. Spieker described how the dead bodies of two teenage children had been found. They had died while a transport was being loaded the previous night, and their bodies had simply been abandoned.[32]

Some of the German engineers started taking photographs of the deportees and the conditions in which they were transported. This led to an order (marked 'Very urgent') on 10 September from General Djemal Pasha that all negatives and copies of such pictures should be handed over within 48 hours. The railway employees were warned: 'All those who do not hand over these photographs will be subject to punishment and judged as having taken photographs on the field of war without authorisation.' Despite this prohibition, on 30 October 1915, Franz Günther, vice-president of the Anatolian Railway (a man who declared that he was appalled by the 'bestial horribleness' of the 'extermination of the Armenians in today's Turkey'), sent his Berlin-based chairman, Arthur Gwinner, a photograph of one of the Armenian railway transports. He wrote: 'Enclosed I send you a picture illustrating the Anatolian Railway as a bearer of culture in Turkey. These are our so-called mutton cars, in which for example 800 human beings are transported in 10 cars.'[33]

On the deportation routes there were transit camps of makeshift tents, which quickly became breeding grounds for disease, taking their toll on the steady stream of thousands of exiled Armenians, especially who had to stay there for any length of time. On 8 September 1915 Dr William Dodd described the revolting conditions in the camps at Eregli and Konia, where sanitary arrangements were non-existent and 'every spot is used for depositing excrement'. The result was dysentery and diarrhoea, while the region in which the camps were placed was 'exceedingly malarial'. The German missionary Sister Paula Schäfer visited Islahiye on 1 December in the same year, and wrote that the transit camp 'is the saddest thing I have ever seen'. Heaps of corpses lay next to tents containing people suffering from severe dysentery in surroundings of 'indescribable filth'. She noted that in just one day 'the burial-commission buried as many as 580 people'. Islahiye camp was open for ten months in 1915 and 1916. Kévorkian estimates that during that time 60,000 deportees died of starvation or typhus there.[34]

In northern Syria there were concentration camps which doubled as transit camps for those on the way to Der Zor. Meskené, between Aleppo and Rakka, was one example. Beatrice Rohner, a Swiss missionary, paid a visit to the camp on 20 April 1916. At that time there were 3,500 Armenian deportees there and over 100 orphans. Starving people were eating raw grass. Hundreds of sick people were left out in the open, 'under the glowing sun'. She wrote that 'I saw desperate ones throw themselves in grave-trenches and beg the grave-diggers to bury them'. On 27 July Consul Rössler passed on information about Meskené to the Imperial Chancellor in Berlin. A Turkish military pharmacist who had been stationed in the camp for six months had said that 'in Meskené alone 55,000 Armenians had been buried'.[35]

The terrible conditions in Rakka were described to Elvesta Leslie by an Armenian woman who had spent a year there as a refugee:

> Many died of starvation and disease. The streets sometimes were lined with children sitting begging, or lying sick. When complaint was made of the condition of the streets, the answer was that they would all be cleaned the next day. The next day the police took all the sick and helpless from the streets and threw them into the Euphrates.[36]

Ras-ul-Ayn concentration camp, north of Der Zor, was the scene of systematic massacres in the spring of 1916. On 6 April Consul Rössler informed the German Embassy that 'the largest part of the 14,000 inmates' of the camp had been killed by 'Circassians and other similar people living nearby'. Three weeks later, having received reliable information from a German who had been visiting the area, he was able to pass on the details to Berlin. Only 2,000 deportees were now left in the camp. Every day, for over a month, 300 to 500 of the Armenians had been taken from the camp and slaughtered after a ten kilometre march. Their bodies were disposed of in a river. A Turkish officer who questioned the district governor about the killings, 'received the calm answer that he was acting under orders'. The butchery was carried out by some Circassian Chechens who had settled in the area. In July Ambassador Wolff-Metternich reported that the Ras-ul-Ayn camp had been evacuated. The remaining Armenians had been sent on in convoys: 'a first transport has been attacked and smashed to pieces while walking towards Der Zor, one can assume that the others have met no better a fate'.[37]

The desert town of Der Zor in northern Syria had been

the destination of the very first deportations from Cilicia. Sister Laura Möhring, a German missionary, visited some Armenians there in early July 1915. She spoke to some villagers from Furnus, near Zeytun, who had reached the town after a four week journey. They had crowded into the large local khan, where they had taken over every possible space. After three weeks there they had run out of money, and were being given very little food by the Turks. On 30 July Consul Rössler reported that there were now 15,000 Armenians in Der Zor 'whose feeding by the government is completely inadequate'. He mentioned that starving people had sold more than thirty children to get money for food. The American Consul wrote to his Ambassador a few days later with identical information, saying that it had been supplied by the governor of Der Zor.[38]

By 26 September 1915, however, Ambassador Morgenthau was surprised to hear from an Armenian visitor that 'the Armenians at Zor were fairly well satisfied, that they have already settled down to business and are earning their living'. As the Ambassador himself noted, these particular deportees 'were the first ones that were sent away and seem to have gotten there without being massacred'.[39] They were helped by the friendly attitude of the local governor, Suad Bey, described by Rössler as 'a humane kind of person' and 'one of the few Turkish officials who tries to mitigate the horrific orders of the government in their implementation'. Amazingly, the police chief in Der Zor, Nerses Kiurdian, was an Armenian who had somehow succeeded in remaining in post. These first Armenians to reach the town established themselves, with characteristic resilience and enterprise, as traders and craftsmen.[40]

Later deportees found things more difficult. Dr Schacht, a captain in the medical corps, reported on the situation in Der Zor in November 1915. A large concentration camp had been established on the fringe of the town: 'On the left bank of the river next to the pontoon bridge masses of dying people have been camped in huts made of foliage.' The local doctor reported a mortality rate of 150-200 people a day. Schacht was deeply shocked by what he found, and declared that 'no linguistic expression can even come close to describing the reality of this human misery; so indescribable are the occurrences here'. He did, however, note that the authorities were carefully cleaning the streets and corners each day, building new residential areas, and distributing money, flour and bread.[41]

By April 1916 the Turkish government policy of concentrating deportees in Der Zor was changed. Henceforth the number of Armenians permitted there would only be the equivalent of 10% of the local population. This meant that at least 13,000 of them would have to be moved on. The Turkish officer who informed Consul Rössler of this new development thought that very few of them would be likely to arrive safely in Mosul. However, the closure of the concentration camps on the way to Der Zor, and the moving on of their inmates, meant that by the end of June the number of deportees in the area around the desert town was approximately 200,000. In early July the kindly governor was replaced by a ruthless hater of Armenians, Salih Zeki Bey. Around 15 July the first of twenty one convoys left Der Zor. Two days later the Armenian clergy and community leaders were arrested. Zeki Bey cleared out the camp and then proceeded to shift the Armenians who had settled in the town. Two thousand Armenian orphans remained in Der Zor in appalling conditions of hunger and neglect. Zeki Bey later had them taken out into the desert where they were either blown up with dynamite or burned alive.[42]

Beyond Der Zor, on the banks of the Khabur River, the

mass killing of deportees began. Hosep Sarkissian was the sole survivor from a convoy of 1,700 people. After walking for several days, they were surrounded by Circassian horsemen, stripped of all their clothes and possessions, and forced to continue for three hours, until they reached a plateau. There they were hacked to pieces by the Circassians, while Zeki Bey stood on a wagon and egged the butchers on. The plateau was surrounded by soldiers to make sure that no one escaped. Hosep hid under a pile of corpses, and waited for three days. Then he crawled out and, disguised as a dervish, eventually made his way to Aleppo.[43] The Armenian journalist and author Aram Andonian estimated that Zeki Bey wiped out 192,750 Armenians in the area around Der Zor between July and December 1916. When the Young Turk leaders were indicted at their trial on 27 April 1919 the figure for those murdered in Zor was set even higher at 195,750. Salih Zeki Bey was tried *in absentia*, accused of 'murder and annihilation, looting, and seizure of property of the Armenians deported to Zor from the various regions of the empire'. The court decided that he had personally taken part in attacks, as well as organising gangs to attack deportees, and helping himself to a share of the loot. Both Muslims and non-Muslims testified against him under oath, and he was sentenced to death on 28 April 1920.[44]

Der Zor has come to have a special resonance for Armenians. On a visit to Der Zor in 1934, Coadjutor Catholicos Papken Guleserian wrote:

We saw the desolate fields where the Armenian people perished, driven there from their paternal homes.

Deir el Zor ... the slaughterhouse of Armenians. A name that brings shivers to Armenians – a shiver that still runs in our nerves like a fever.[45]

A more recent visitor, the photographer Bardig Kouyoumdjian, grandson of a Genocide survivor, also attempts to put this feeling into words: 'In the subconscious of the Armenian that I am, this name, Der Zor, is the symbol of genocide, a trace left on the surface of the planet, the cemetery of a people.'[46] But perhaps the most effective expressions of all are in the folk laments collected by Verjiné Svazlian:

The desert of Der-Zor was covered with mist,
Oh, mother! Oh, mother! Our condition was lamentable,
People and grass were stained with blood,
Armenians dying for the sake of faith!

They pitched tents in the Der-Zor desert,
They gathered Armenians in the desert,
They dropped the remaining into the rivers
Or brutally burned them with sulphur.

They gathered the Armenians in a cave,
They covered them with lime, set fire and burned them,
Oh, mother! Oh, mother! Our condition was lamentable,
At the time we were in the desert of Der-Zor.

I got up in the morning: the sun was shining.
The Chechens, seated, were oiling their guns,
Mothers and fathers were crying their hearts out,
Armenians dying for the sake of faith!

I fell, wounded, in the desert of Der-Zor,
There is no doctor to dress my wound,
Oh, mother! Oh mother! Our condition was lamentable,
At the time we were in the desert of Der-Zor.

I rotted and remained in the desert of Der-Zor,
I remained and became a meal for the crows,
Oh, mother! Oh, mother! Our condition was lamentable,
At the time we were in the desert of Der-Zor.

The bridge of Der-Zor is narrow, impassable,
The water is bloody; you can't drink a single cup,
The Armenian deportee cannot come back,
Armenians dying for the sake of faith![47]

[1] Leslie A. Davis, *The Slaughterhouse Province: An American Diplomat's Report on the Armenian Genocide, 1915-1917*, edited by Susan K. Blair (New Rochelle, New York: Aristide D. Caratzas, Publisher , 1989), p.87.

[2] Toroyan and Essayan, *L'Agonie d'un people*, p.92.

[3] Toroyan and Essayan, *L'Agonie d'un people*, p.89 (my translation).

[4] Dadrian, *To the Desert*, pp.294-5.

[5] Sarafian, *United States Official Records*, pp.330-2; C.S. Graber, *Caravans to Oblivion: The Armenian Genocide 1915* (New York, John Wiley & Sons, 1996).

[6] Gust, *The Armenian Genocide*, p.639.

[7] Sarafian, *United States Official Records*, p.687; Kévorkian, *The Armenian Genocide*, pp.344, 376; Barton, *'Turkish Atrocities'*, p.82.

[8] Gust, *The Armenian Genocide*, p.350.

[9] Gust, *The Armenian Genocide*, pp.345,633.

[10] Barton, *'Turkish Atrocities'*, pp.24-5.

[11] Jacobsen, *Diaries*, pp.164,182,184,188.

[12] Morley, *Marsovan 1915*, p.51.

[13] Fethiye Çetin, *My Grandmother: A Memoir* (London: Verso, 2008), p.102.

[14] Riggs, *Days of Tragedy*, p.96; Kévorkian, *The Armenian Genocide*, p.314; Jacobsen, *Diaries*, p.82.

[15] Jacobsen, *Diaries*, p.122.

[16] Gust, *The Armenian Genocide*, pp.281,521.

[17] Dadrian and Akçam, *Judgment at Istanbul*, p.275.

[18] Gust, *The Armenian Genocide*, p.260.

[19] Üngör, *The Making of Modern Turkey*, pp.79-81; Kévorkian, *The Armenian Genocide*, pp.491, 502, 564-5; Dadrian and Akçam, *Judgment at Istanbul*, pp.208,280.

[20] Kévorkian, *The Armenian Genocide*, p.346; Svazlian, *The Armenian Genocide*, p.82.

[21] Svazlian, *The Armenian Genocide*, p.98.

[22] Kévorkian, *The Armenian Genocide*, pp.346-8; Gust, *The Armenian Genocide*, pp.470-2; Robert H. Hewsen, 'The Historical Geography of Baghesh/Bitlis and Taron/Mush' in Richard G. Hovannisian (editor), *Armenian Baghesh/Bitlis and Taron/Mush* (Costa Mesa, California: Mazda Publishers, 2001), p.58.

[23] Bryce and Toynbee, *The Treatment of Armenians*, pp.520-7; Svazlian, *The Armenian Genocide*, p.464.

[24] Franz Werfel, *The Forty Days of Musa Dagh*, with an introduction by Peter Sourian (New York: Carroll & Graf Publishers, 2002), p.xv; Edward Minasian, *Musa Dagh: A chronicle of the Armenian Genocide factor in the subsequent suppression, by the intervention of the United States government, of the movie based on Franz Werfel's The Forty Days of Musa Dagh* (San Francisco, California: the author, 2007).

[25] Simon Payaslian, 'The Armenian Resistance at Shabin-Karahisar, 1915' in Richard G. Hovannisian (editor), *Armenian Sebastia/Sivas and Lesser Armenia* (Costa Mesa, California: Mazda Publishers, 2004), pp.399-426.

[26] Walker, *Armenia*, pp.159,163-4.

[27] Sarafian, *United States Official Records*, p.199.

[28] Eberhard Count Wolffskeel Von Reichenberg, *Zeitoun, Mousa Dagh, Ourfa: Letters on the Armenian Genocide*, second edition, edited by Hilmar Kaiser (Princeton, New Jersey: Gomidas Institute, 2004), p.21.

[29] Carlos Bedrossian, 'Urfa's Last Stand, 1915' in Hovannissian, *Armenian Tigranakert/Diarbekir and Edessa/Urfa*, pp.487-96; Kévorkian, *The Armenian Genocide*, pp.617-20.

[30] Barton, *'Turkish Atrocities'*, p.112.

[31] Bryce and Toynbee, *The Treatment of Armenians*, p.434.

[32] Gust, *The Armenian Genocide*, p.356.

[33] Gust, *The Armenian Genocide*, pp.385-6; Kévorkian, *The Armenian Genocide*, p.579.

[34] Sarafian, *United States Official Records*, pp.252-3; Gust, *The Armenian Genocide*, p.534; Kévorkian, *The Armenian Genocide*, p.633.

[35] Gust, *The Armenian Genocide*, pp.605,608.

[36] Barton, *'Turkish Atrocities'*, p.113.

[37] Gust, *The Armenian Genocide*, pp.573,581-2;601.

[38] Gust, *The Armenian Genocide*, pp.275,313; Sarafian, *United States Official Records*, p.169.

[39] Morgenthau, *United States Diplomacy: Diaries*, p.340.

[40] Gust, *The Armenian Genocide*, p.581; Kévorkian, *The Armenian Genocide*, p.663.

41 Gust, *The Armenian Genocide*, pp.463-4.

42 Gust, *The Armenian Genocide*, pp.581,608; Kévorkian, *The Armenian Genocide*, pp.663-7.

43 Gust, *The Armenian Genocide*, pp.674-5.

44 Kévorkian, *The Armenian Genocide*, p.668; Dadrian and Akçam, *Judgment at Istanbul*, pp.222-3.

45 Vatche Ghazarian (editor), *The Life and Work of Coadjutor Catholicos Papken Guleserian* (Waltham, Massachusetts: Mayreni Publishing, 2000), p.69.

46 Bardig Kouyoumdjian and Christine Siméone, *Deir-es-Zor: Sur les traces du genocide arménien de 1915* (Arles: Actes Sud, 2005), p.33 (my translation).

47 Svazlian, *The Armenian Genocide*, pp.569,571-3,575.

EPILOGUE

Each visit to the Armenian Genocide Memorial and Museum in Yerevan has touched my heart in a different way. Once it was seeing the single skull of a Genocide victim: a reminder that each number in those horrifying statistics represents an individual, made in the image and likeness of God to love and be loved. On another occasion it was Jansem's soul-searing paintings that proved almost unbearable to look at. And then there was the time when the photographs of Western Armenian poets and authors killed in 1915 brought a sudden awareness of the brutal snuffing out of an extraordinary cultural renaissance. Most moving of all, however, were the people who came to place a flower and say a prayer by the perpetual flame at the centre of the Memorial: remembering with quiet dignity the jagged gaps torn in their families by the great evil that the Ottoman Armenians suffered a hundred years ago.

The Welsh word *hiraeth* is difficult to translate into English. It means a heart-wrenching longing for a place or a person or a time that can never be again. The Armenians have a word which goes even deeper: *garod* – a combination of *hiraeth* with the results of centuries of oppression, suffering and loss. For those who survived the Genocide that sense of *garod* was particularly heartbreaking. It shattered the sanity of Komitas, the gentle composer and collector of songs. It haunted the paintings of Arshile Gorky, and may ultimately have been a factor in his suicide. The Genocide left an indelible impact on all those who somehow came through it.

Tonakan Abraham Tonakan was twenty two years old when the Genocide swept away his village in the plain of Mush, destroying almost all his extended family. His words reflect the impact of this unforgettable experience, which was with him for the rest of his days:

Sometimes I fly with my memories to Moosh ...
When I begin thinking, it seems to me, that I'll go mad, when I remember my father's house, my relatives, our huge yard surrounded with tall poplars and the storks knitting their nests in them every spring ... The well, the barn, the tonir-house, the cool wood, which was the continuation of our yard and the summer pastures ... the hazelnut trees, the nuts, the wild honey combs with bekmez, kamads madsoun, the New Year table garnish – oleaster, the dried fruits (apricot, apple, pear, plum) and raisins and the baghardj, kneaded and baked with my mother's righteous hands. At Easter or on my birthday the luck button hidden in the baghardj. I remember with a deep grief, one by one, name by name, I remember our dear ones who did not even have a grave, who were not buried, my lost and forever gone brothers, their wives and children. My innocent sisters, the young women who, escaping the brutal askyars threw themselves into the Euphrates-Mourat River; which one should I

mention, which one should I deplore. ... I want to find
and deliver to the holy earth the unburied bones of my
relatives; I want to take out from the bed of the
Euphrates-Mourat River my sisters' and cousins sacred
relics, who, for their honour, threw themselves into the
river. I want to tour the whole world, to search and find
my forty-eight lost kinsfolk ...[1]

The anguish of *garod* can be overwhelming.

And yet, Armenians are intensely practical and down-to-
earth, with amazing resilience and creativity. Their most
potent symbol is the *khatchar* – the Cross of suffering that
becomes a Cross of victory, sprouting leaves, bearing fruit,
transformed into the Tree of Life. Whenever I see an
Armenian mother cradling her Armenian child, or hear
young people speaking the glorious Armenian language;
whenever I watch a cheerful crowd of Armenians dancing as
only Armenians can; whenever I'm lifted up to heaven by
the ethereal music of the *Badarak* (the Armenian Liturgy),
my heart rejoices in the knowledge that Talaat, Enver and
their brutal henchmen failed. They may have bathed
Western Armenia in blood and tears and misery, creating
through Genocide their 'Armenia without Armenians'.
However, they did not crush the spirit of this extraordinary
people – the oldest Christian nation in the world.

---

[1] Svazlian, *The Armenian Genocide*, pp.96-7.

SOME FURTHER READING ...

Taner Akçam, *A Shameful Act: The Armenian Genocide and the Question of Responsibility* (Metropolitan Books)

Aram Andonian, *Exile Trauma and Death: On the road to Chankiri with Komitas Vartabed*, edited by Rita Soulahian Kuyumjian (Gomidas Institute and Tekeyan Cultural Association)

Grigoris Balakian, *Armenian Golgotha: A Memoir of the Armenian Genocide, 1915-1918* (Alfred A. Knopf)

Peter Balakian, *The Burning Tigris: The Armenian Genocide* (William A. Heinemann)

Fethiye Çetin, *My Grandmother: A Memoir* (Verso)

Vahan Dadrian, *To the Desert: Pages from My Diary* (Gomidas Institute)

Raymond Kévorkian, *The Armenian Genocide: A Complete History* (I.B. Tauris)

Donald E. Miller and Lorna Touryan Miller, *Survivors: An Oral History of the Armenian Genocide* (University of California Press)

Henry Morgenthau, *Ambassador Morgenthau's Story: A Personal Account of the Armenian Genocide* (Cosimo Classics)

Henry H. Riggs, *Days of Tragedy in Armenia: Personal Experiences in Harpoot, 1915-1917* (Gomidas Institute)

Carmarthen to Karabagh:
a Welsh discovery of Armenia
by Patrick Thomas
www.carreg-gwalch.com